Y0-BRH-070

Biliteracy and Globalization

Mixed Sources
Product group from well-managed
forests and other controlled sources
www.fsc.org   Cert no. TT-COC-2082
© 1996 Forest Stewardship Council

BILINGUAL EDUCATION AND BILINGUALISM
Series Editors: Professor Nancy H. Hornberger, *University of Pennsylvania, Philadelphia, USA* and *Professor Colin Baker, University of Wales, Bangor, Wales, Great Britain*

Recent Books in the Series

Beyond the Beginnings: Literacy Interventions for Upper Elementary English Language Learners
Angela Carrasquillo, Stephen B. Kucer and Ruth Abrams

Bilingualism and Language Pedagogy
Janina Brutt-Griffler and Manka Varghese (eds)

Language Learning and Teacher Education: A Sociocultural Approach
Margaret R. Hawkins (ed.)

The English Vernacular Divide: Postcolonial Language Politics and Practice
Vaidehi Ramanathan

Bilingual Education in South America
Anne-Marie de Mejía (ed.)

Teacher Collaboration and Talk in Multilingual Classrooms
Angela Creese

Words and Worlds: World Languages Review
F. Martí, P. Ortega, I. Idiazabal, A. Barreña, P. Juaristi, C. Junyent, B. Uranga and E. Amorrortu

Language and Aging in Multilingual Contexts
Kees de Bot and Sinfree Makoni

Foundations of Bilingual Education and Bilingualism (4th edn)
Colin Baker

Bilingual Minds: Emotional Experience, Expression and Representation
Aneta Pavlenko (ed.)

Raising Bilingual-Biliterate Children in Monolingual Cultures
Stephen J. Caldas

Language, Space and Power: A Critical Look at Bilingual Education
Samina Hadi-Tabassum

Developing Minority Language Resources
Guadalupe Valdés, Joshua A. Fishman, Rebecca Chávez and William Pérez

Language Loyalty, Language Planning and Language Revitalization: Recent Writings and Reflections from Joshua A. Fishman
Nancy H. Hornberger and Martin Pütz (eds)

Language Loyalty, Continuity and Change: Joshua A. Fishman's Contributions to International Sociolinguistics
Ofelia Garcia, Rakhmiel Peltz and Harold Schiffman

Bilingual Education: An Introductory Reader
Ofelia García and Colin Baker (eds)

Disinventing and Reconstituting Languages
Sinfree Makoni and Alastair Pennycook (eds)

Language and Identity in a Dual Immersion School
Kim Potowski

Bilingual Education in China: Practices, Policies and Concepts
Anwei Feng (ed.)

English Learners Left Behind: Standardized Testing as Language Policy
Kate Menken

For more details of these or any other of our publications, please contact:
Multilingual Matters, Frankfurt Lodge, Clevedon Hall,
Victoria Road, Clevedon, BS21 7HH, England
http://www.multilingual-matters.com

BILINGUAL EDUCATION AND BILINGUALISM 67
Series Editors: Nancy H. Hornberger and Colin Baker

Biliteracy and Globalization
English Language Education in India

Viniti Vaish

MULTILINGUAL MATTERS LTD
Clevedon • Buffalo • Toronto

To Papa, who did not live to see this book published

Library of Congress Cataloging in Publication Data
Vaish, Viniti
Biliteracy and Globalization: English Language Education in India / Viniti Vaish.
Bilingual Education and Bilingualism: 67
Includes bibliographical references and index.
1. English language–Study and teaching–India. 2. English language–Social
aspects–India. 3. Education, Bilingual–India. 4. Globalization–Economic
aspects–India. 5. Language policy–India. I. Title.
PE1068.I4V35 2008
428.007'054–dc22   2007040069

British Library Cataloguing in Publication Data
A catalogue entry for this book is available from the British Library.

ISBN-13: 978-1-84769-033-3 (hbk)
ISBN-13: 978-1-84769-032-6 (pbk)

Multilingual Matters Ltd
UK: Frankfurt Lodge, Clevedon Hall, Victoria Road, Clevedon BS21 7HH.
USA: UTP, 2250 Military Road, Tonawanda, NY 14150, USA.
Canada: UTP, 5201 Dufferin Street, North York, Ontario M3H 5T8, Canada.

Copyright © 2008 Viniti Vaish.

All rights reserved. No part of this work may be reproduced in any form or by any
means without permission in writing from the publisher.

The policy of Multilingual Matters/Channel View Publications is to use papers that
are natural, renewable and recyclable products, made from wood grown in
sustainable forests. In the manufacturing process of our books, and to further support
our policy, preference is given to printers that have FSC and PEFC Chain of Custody
certification. The FSC and/or PEFC logos will appear on those books where full
certification has been granted to the printer concerned.

Typeset by Datapage International Ltd.
Printed and bound in Great Britain by the Cromwell Press Ltd.

Contents

Preface

I arrived in West Lafayette, Indiana, on 15 September, 1987. That was the year Alan Bloom had published *The Closing of the American Mind*, which was on the lists of all the book clubs I tried to join. The central thesis of the book, that a curriculum should include the traditional canon of Western culture starting from the Greeks and Romans because an 'openness' to all types of literature and ideas in American schools had made young Americans confused about what is really good literature, was provocative. According to Bloom (1987) this 'openness' had actually resulted in closing the American mind. Bloom's idea was the antithesis of Said's (1978) *Orientalism*, which most English literature students in developing countries are familiar with, and which attacks this very canon. Said's contention is that colonial empires were founded and hegemonized on the basis of the superiority of Greek and Roman origins of Western culture.

When I described Bloom's controversial ideas to my father in New Delhi in one of my phone conversations, he remarked in perfect Indian English, 'हाँ (yes), that means that these Americans are like Indians only. The only problem is they don't know how to speak English'. As I had been hired by Purdue University as a teaching assistant to teach Rhetoric and Composition in the English Department, he had some evidence for his second contention. The first was based on the fact that any society that can live with glaring contradictions must be like India.

The India I left in 1987, at the age of 23, had a socialist economy where the middle class had elevated financial resourcefulness and managing scarcity to an art. It was not unusual for women to open presents carefully so that they could use the wrapping paper again and give children dough to play with before making roti instead of buying plasticine (now called playdoh). It was an India where color TV was just a few years old, there was one government owned channel and all the advertisements on TV were stills. 'Readymade' clothes, i.e. mass produced garments, which no Indian trusted, as most people used tailors, had just entered the market. When I was in high school, there was national pride in the fact that the Coke company was disallowed from doing business in India and an Indian Campa Cola was launched.

I lived in Philadelphia from 1989 onwards as a member of the Penn community and a student at the Graduate School of Education. This melting pot experience, called hybridity in postcolonial theory, greatly influenced me. The strongest influence in my graduate experience was that of Nancy H. Hornberger and her work in Peru. The years she spent in Peru and the way she lived in a rural community by participating in their work was inspiring. Equally inspiring were friendships with my colleagues who were working on language in education issues in Ecuador, Arkansas and Indonesia. I only brought a rudimentary knowledge of Said with me from India. It was attending seminars at Penn by members of the South Asia, Anthropology and History departments, along with the enormous resources of the Van Pelt library that made this rudimentary interest into the conceptual framework for my dissertation.

The dissertation that emerged from this experience was Vidyashakti: Literacy and Empowerment in India, the Continua of Biliteracy in Action (Vaish, 2004). In this text I compared two schools with different bilingual programs: the Rajkiya Sarvodaya Kanya Vidyalaya (RSKV) and the Nagar Nigam Bal Vidyalaya (NNBV). In an attempt to tell this story to a wider audience I have used only the RSKV in this book, as this is the school that includes English substantially in its curriculum. Another difference between the two texts is that my dissertation was only on the primary wing of the RSKV and the NNBV. In this book I have also analyzed data from the high school of the RSKV as I wanted to make comments on the life pathways of the graduating students after 12 years of English-medium education.

When I started my fieldwork in December 2000, India had been globalizing for nearly 10 years. In this India billboards for foreign brands like Benetton and Coke (yes, the company finally made it into the Indian market) jostled with signs for the Rapidex English Speaking Course, which promised to inject fluency in English and confidence into Indians and at the same time open enchanted doors of opportunity. There was a rash of cyber cafes all over the face of New Delhi, most of them operating on personal generators, as New Delhi does not generate enough electricity for its 13 million inhabitants.

In 1987, when I moved to the USA, if there was news about India in *The New York Times* by Barbara Crosette, it was usually about floods and earthquakes. In 2007 *The International Herald Tribune,* which includes articles from *The New York Times*, reports on India as a developing country with enormous potential and as the center of the world's outsourcing businesses because of its growing English-knowing middle class. The international image of India has changed in the last two decades from an elephantine socialist economy to one of the fastest growing 'Asian tiger' economies; the role of the increasing pool of English-knowing bilinguals has been central to this change in image.

I currently work as an Assistant Professor in Singapore's National Institute of Education. The Center for Research in Pedagogy and Practice, to which I am attached, conducts research on the government-run school system of Singapore. Thus this book has given my evenings and weekends windows with which to explore other avenues, to return the gaze towards home. It has also been interesting to compare these two postcolonies – India and Singapore – that have taken different pathways in their economy, politics and bilingual educational policy after independence from the British. But that is another story...

Viniti Vaish
Singapore

Introduction

This book is about how the majority of Indians learn and use English in the national school system based on recent changes in language in education brought about by globalization. Specifically the positionality of English has changed in the Three Language Formula (TLF), which is India's language in education policy. English was offered as a second or third language in secondary school; however, due to tremendous demand it is now offered as a medium of instruction from nursery itself in dual-medium schools. Within the field of bilingual education, the book is about biliteracy, a term defined by Hornberger (2003), and how the contested sites of biliteracy in India can be documented, explored and evaluated in a globalizing postcolonial context. The stance of this book leans towards English as an empowering vocational skill in a globalizing economy.

Specifically this study asks: how are the urban disadvantaged taught English in India? What is the nature of pedagogic practice in primary and high school classes in government schools? What are the attitudes towards Hindi and English amongst this cohort? What are the text types that such children like to produce and how do they use English? What are the professional aspirations of these children? Is the English they have learned in their 12 years of school adequate for the demands of the globalizing workforce, which increasingly demands an English-knowing and often English-speaking worker? What more needs to be done in terms of teacher training, pedagogical reform, text book creation and building teacher capacity to sustain the empowering role of English in today's India?

This story is set in the city of New Delhi. With a population of about 13 million in 2001 (http://www.censusindia.net/results/provindia1.html), Delhi is a vast capital city with four main languages: Hindi, Punjabi, English and Urdu. The road signs, as shown on the cover of this book, are in four scripts: Devanagari, Gurmukhi, Roman and Arabic. This road sign shows a somewhat unknown road, called Sir Edmund Hillary Marg, named after the mountaineer who was the first to scale Mount Everest. The first line on this road sign is in Devanagari, then Roman, then Gurmukhi and finally in the Arabic scripts. The word Marg is Hindi for Road and that appears even in the English name. This semiotic symbol tells many stories: that Hindi is the most powerful language of Delhi followed by

English; then the large Punjabi community is acknowledged and finally, the Muslim minority is marginalized at the very bottom. The fact that the Hindi word 'Marg' meaning 'road' appears even in the Roman/English line is indicative of how English has been hybridized or 'tandoorified' in the linguistic space of India.

The Indian Constitution lists Delhi as a Union Territory, which is an area too small to be a fully fledged state. The boundaries of Delhi actually include 199 villages and 32 towns, though it is considered one city. It is one of the most developed parts of India with a literacy rate of 81.8%, which compares favorably with the national average of 65.4% (eCensus of India, 2001). From a population of about 11 million in 1991, around 8 million people speak Hindi. The next most widely spoken language is Punjabi, with about 750,000 speakers. Only 3622 people in Delhi listed English as their mother tongue in the 1991 census (Bose, 1998). However, most people who have a secondary school education will be able to understand some English. There is also an Urdu-speaking Muslim minority in Delhi.

Delhi has a massive school system that services its current population of 13 million. In 2004–05, about 93,000 teachers were teaching more than 3 million children enrolled in over 2500 schools. In 2003–04 the Delhi government spent Rs. 927 per child on education as against the national average of Rs. 749. It is estimated that 75% of all primary school children in Delhi and 50% of children enrolled in secondary and high school use the government school system. As mentioned earlier, close to 82% of Delhi's population is literate – higher than the national average of 65.4%. At the same time 6.4% of children in the 6–10 age group and 7% of children in the 11–14 age group in Delhi are out of school (Delhi: Human Development Report, 2006). Delhi has about 400,000 child workers and another 100,000 street children who are not in school (Govinda, 2002). I have seen them working in wayside tea shops, as shoeshine boys and as rag pickers, when I was child going to school in Delhi; and I see them now when I go out as a researcher to collect data.

The Rajkiya Sarvodaya Kanya Vidyalaya (RSKV) or State Sarovodya Girls' School of East Vinod Nagar, which is briefly described in Vaish (2005), is the school described in detail in this book. It is part of a chain of RSKVs run by the Delhi Administration. *Kanya* in the title means girl and the RSKVs are girls' schools, but many of them enroll boys from Class 1 till Class 3. The word 'Sarvodaya' roughly translates as 'welfare for all' and is taken from the writings of Mohandas Karmachand Gandhi (1869–1948), on whose ideology these schools are founded. The RSKV that I have been observing is located in East Vinod Nagar, a disadvantaged neighborhood. Outside the principal's office is a board which says in English 'Motto: Not Me but You'. The principal has a sign on her desk that says: कृपया हिन्दी का उपयोग करें, meaning 'Please use Hindi'. These schools charge a fee of Rs. 15 per term (US$1 is equivalent to Rs. 50). From 1 July 2000, the Delhi Administration allocated Rs. 400 per year per child for free text books and school bags.

In each class the children go through three tests. The session begins in July (on the first of July every year the children enter a new grade) and they have the first test in September, the second in December and the third in May. In Classes 1, 2 and 3 promotion is automatic as long as the student shows 75% attendance. After Class 3 the weak students may be held back. The school has a small library and computer room. The secondary school has weekly access to the computer room and when there is 'load shedding' or a power outage in Delhi and the children cannot switch on the computers, they are taught 'theory'.

The RSKV in East Vinod Nagar has two sections for each class, one Hindi and the other English medium; some other RSKVs are totally English medium. Until 1999 the whole school was English medium, but the principal felt the children could not cope with the English medium so she made one section Hindi medium for the weaker students. For the English-medium classes, Science, Maths and English are in English and Hindi and Social Studies (SSt) are in Hindi. For the Hindi-medium sections Science and Maths are also in Hindi and the children study English as a second language thrice a week. The teachers of the A and B sections of one class are considered 'partners' and divide the subjects amongst themselves.

From Class 6 to 12 all the students have to take a third language, which is taught every day for 40 minutes. This is part of the TLF, which is India's language-in-education policy. The RSKV offers a choice of Sanskrit, Urdu and Punjabi as third languages. Generally the Hindu students take Sanskrit, Muslim students Urdu, and Sikh/Punjabi students Punjabi. I have yet to come across a student in the school who has no religion or is an atheist. The home language of most of the children is Hindi though some speak either Punjabi, or a dialect of Hindi. The Hindu children are familiar with Sanskrit due to active participation in their local temples. The Muslim children speak mainly Urdu and Punjabi at home but they are familiar with Arabic as the language of the Koran.

This model of bilingual education is difficult to slot into models of international prototypes. What the RSKV calls the 'English-medium' stream comes closest to what Baker (2006) describes as a 50–50 dual language program. However, Baker points out that in most dual language programs there is a fairly strict separation of languages in the classroom. For instance Math might be taught in Spanish on Tuesdays and Thursdays, but in English on Mondays, Wednesdays and Fridays. In the RSKV, as Chapters 6 and 7 will show, there are no such boundaries; on the contrary pedagogic practices encourage border crossings and dissolving of isoglosses.

Also, when we add the Hindi-medium stream to this along with the third language, which is Urdu, Punjabi or Sanskrit, then this can no longer be called a dual language program. Even in those RSKVs where there is no Hindi-medium stream, there is a problem of how the third language can be reconciled within a dual language program, as actually 3 languages are being taught in the national school system of India. Of these 2 are usually taught as media of instruction and one as a subject. Thus though bilingual education in India has something in common with dual language programs, especially in terms of educational outcomes, which are optimal bilingualism and biliteracy, I think it best to call this model its indigenous name: Three Language Formula or TLF. Interestingly this term has no Hindi equivalent and I have always heard it being referred to in English.

The RSKVs are based on a concept called 'Sarvodaya', meaning universal welfare, which was popularized by Mohandas Karamchand Gandhi (1869–1948), who was a freedom fighter and social scientist and is considered the father of the Indian nation. The concept of Sarovodaya will be problematized in this book, specifically in the last chapter, which is about biliteracy and the workplace. Gandhi envisioned an education system that would develop both the spirit and the intellect of the child and in the end provide empowering opportunity for employment and self-sufficiency. Bilingual education in India, which includes the mother tongue of the child, the language of religion and spirituality, and the language of the globalizing workforce that can be commodified, must be seen in terms of Sarvodaya.

The parents of the children in the RSKV are involved in occupations like carpentry, rickshaw pulling, selling produce on the streets or domestic work. At best they have jobs in government offices where they could be peons, clerks or security personnel. Sweta Tomar, one of the brightest girls in RSKV's English-medium Grade 5 (2004), is the daughter of a meter reader at the Delhi Jal (Water) Board. Her father, who goes to work on a bicycle, earns about Rs. 4000 per month (80 USD). In this community there is a high premium placed on English language learning and Sweta's father removed his son from the RSKV high school and put him in a public school because he was not satisfied with the English language teaching. Some of the parents are migrant workers and work only when they can find jobs. The fathers of the children in this school are likely to have a secondary school level education in Hindi. Many of the mothers have no formal schooling.

I received permission from The Directorate of Education to observe classes in four government schools in the East Vinod Nagar area of Delhi in December 1999. I chose two schools, one of which was the RSKV mentioned herein, for my dissertation. Though the dissertation was submitted in 2003, I have continued my research in the RSKV. In 2003 and then again in 2006 my permit was renewed by the Directorate of Education. I visited the RSKV two to four times a year for about two weeks each time. In each visit, besides observing classes, I also interviewed teachers, parents, policymakers and students. My data are in the form of audio and video files, field notes, photos and artifacts from the class in the form of student work and text books with students' notes written in. The structure of each visit was open ended. In each of my visits the principal, Mrs. S, assigned me the teachers she thought I could observe. Each class is 50 min long. When I could not observe any of the teachers assigned to me, Mrs. S did not mind my sitting in the staff room or in the verandah on sunny winter mornings to interview teachers. My periodic presence in the RSKV is taken for granted now and most of the teachers ignore me and carry on with their work.

From January 2000 till December 2006 I observed a total of 26 lessons in all the grades of the RSKV for a varying number of hours (a double period is nearly 2 hours; revision classes don't have a set time). These include all the English classes from 1 to 12, except nursery, which was added in 2004. This data set of 26 lessons includes a few Hindi classes, which I observed to provide a comparative perspective on language learning. Also, I have observed Science, Math and Social Studies classes in English. Though my primary goal was to observe all the English classes from Grades 1 till 12, which I achieved, I also wanted to observe each subject being taught in both languages, which was not possible. Thus, except for the Math classes for Grade 5, which I managed to observe in both English and Hindi medium streams, all the other lessons are stand alone. All names in this book are pseudonyms except when referring to senior bureaucrats.

I interviewed the teacher immediately after her lesson or the very next day. Interviews with students were conducted when they are not having class and with parents outside school. In total there are 40 interviews with parents, teachers, students and policymakers, each ranging from half an hour to about one hour. Most people, except policymakers and some students, were interviewed more than once. Within these 40 interviews there is a subset of oral and written unstructured interviews that I conducted with Grade 12 in December of 2006. From 19 December till 1 January 2007 there were no classes taking place in the RSKV and the principal allowed me to spend a few hours with Grade 12 every day for two weeks. I used this opportunity to talk to the students mainly about their attitudes to English but also about their personal literacy practices at home. In this section of the total database of interviews there are about 10 hours of oral and written interviews, the results of which are reported in Chapter 5.

This book is a critical ethnography. As such there are numerous tensions inherent in the data analysis. The tension that needs to be emphasized in this introduction is between my background and that of the students I have been observing. Though I come from a middle-class home, the languages – Hindi, English, Sanskrit and Punjabi – and the cultures of my home are not dissimilar to those of the children in the RSKV. No doubt the use of English in my home is greater than in theirs but I have always felt connected to them because we have grown up in the same city with a similar cultural background. More importantly the students, teachers and parents have felt connected to me through all that they have shared.

The reader will encounter numerous other tensions throughout this book: for instance pedagogic practice in government schools in India does not inculcate communicative competence in English, which is the demand of the workplace. Then why have I valorized these pedagogies as culturally contextualized in the 'enunciative space' in which they are occurring? If English taught in the government school system is empowering, as I have claimed it is, then why do students have to supplement this English with training packages in communicative competence outside of school? A similar question confronts the reader regarding globalization: is English language education in India training young people for the grunt work of rich countries? Does globalization deny jobs to workers in rich countries by transferring them to the developing world? I have grappled with these tensions in the course of writing this book and the conclusion explores possible resolutions, although by no means does it offer any solutions.

In the field of the Sociology of Education there are studies demonstrating that social class and not school reform is the main reason for differential academic achievement and life pathways. However there are equally convincing studies that point towards school reform that can break the deterministic constraints of social class (Hannum & Fuller, 2006). This book is a story about bottom-up reform in India's language in education policy, which is helping the urban disadvantaged break the rigid cycle of social reproduction in which the daughter of a cook remains a cook. Sociolinguists who have been writing about the divisive nature of English in India will, no doubt, be unhappy with my study. However, despite the dreary warehouse-like buildings of government schools and the enormous challenges facing ELT in India, I see exciting changes and hear uplifting stories. I wish to emphasize the latter.

Chapter 1

English as a Language of Decolonization

Administratively decolonization refers to the dismantling of colonial machinery and the departure of the colonizer in a grand or gory manner. For instance the spectacle of the British leaving Hong Kong and handing the territory over to China at midnight on 1 July 1997 was performed on the world stage with the pomp of a great Empire leaving in a dignified fashion. The exit from India of the British Empire in 1947, on the other hand, was bloody. The 'divide and rule' policy of the British was successful in dismembering South Asia into Pakistan, India and Bangladesh. The birth of these nations left millions dead in rioting between Hindus and Muslims, a past that these three countries have re-enacted since 1947 in smaller wars and daily border skirmishes. The foundation of the divorce between these countries was linguistic: Urdu in the Arabic script for Muslims in Pakistan versus Hindi in Devanagari for Hindus in India.

Decolonization as a psychological process for a nation is more complex. In the case of Africa decolonization has substituted neocolonialism in place of Empire. Young (2001) defines Nkrumah's idea of neocolonialism as colonization through institutions like the World Bank, the IMF and the Summer Institute of Linguistics, which try to Christianize indigenous populations and make them indebted through financial aid. 'Neocolonialism is … the worst form of imperialism. For those who practice it, it means power without responsibility and for those who suffer from it, it means exploitation without redress' (Kwame Nkrumah, in Young, 2001: xi). This system is supported by an indigenous Western-educated elite that colludes with the ex-colonial masters for its own benefit.

Young's critique of Nkrumah's term neocolonialism is that it does not provide agency and voice to the colonized. He writes, 'His stress on a continuing neocolonial dominance has the disadvantage of suggesting a powerlessness and passivity which underestimates what has been achieved since independence, including the independence movements themselves, perpetuating stereotypes of helplessness even while it implies sympathy, and reinforcing assumptions of western hegemony with the third world being portrayed as its homogeneous eternal victim' (Young,

2001: 48). I think India is an illustration of how neocolonialism has been avoided due to Gandhi's unique methods of resistance, which challenged linguistic and other forms of imperialism, and will be discussed in detail later in this chapter.

The first half of this chapter is somewhat descriptive in nature as here I map the linguistic terrain of independent India in the form of a country case study. Starting with a documentation of the major and minor languages, or Scheduled and Non-Scheduled languages, as they are called in the Indian Constitution, I go on to explain the current national language policy and subsequently present the Three Language Formula (TLF), which is India's language-in-education policy. In the second more analytical half of this chapter I discuss the politics of Hindi as a national language and Gandhi's idea of Hindustani. Also, the issue of media of instruction in the debates on national education will be described as an illustration of the processes of decolonization that have, to a large extent, prevented the stranglehold of neocolonialism. Finally I show how the TLF is changing due to the impact of globalization and the demand for English. Attitudes towards the three languages in the TLF and their economic/cultural capital are illustrated through the 'subaltern speak' of Ram Nivas.

India: A Case Study

With 114 languages and a population in the 2001 census of just over one billion, India presents a fascinating case study for scholars of language in education and society. The census presents a more homogeneous picture of linguistic diversity in India than is the reality. For instance the Central Institute of Indian Languages finds that 'Over 1652 languages belonging to four different language families are spoken in India' (http://www.ciil.org). Annamalai (2001: 35) comments that India 'is functionally multilingual with forty-seven languages used in education as medium, eighty-seven in press, seventy-one in radio, thirteen in cinema and thirteen in state-level administration'. The decennial household census of India, one of the largest door-to-door household censuses in the world, has not yet tabulated all the results of the 2001 census at the time that this book is being written. Thus the language data presented in this case study are from both the 1991 and the 2001 censuses.

The 114 languages of India show immense philological diversity and consequently present a challenge for the national school system, which has to grapple with the schism between home language and media of instruction. This diversity is represented in Table 1.1 (http://www.censusindia.net/results/provindia1.html).

Table 1.1 Family-wise grouping of the 114 languages

Language family	Number of languages	% of total population
Indo-European		
Indo-Aryan	19	75.28
Germanic	1	0.02
Dravidian	17	22.53
Austro-Asiatic	14	1.13
Tibeto-Burmese	62	0.97
Semito-Hamitic	1	0.01
Total	114	99.94

The Constitution of India divides these 114 languages into Scheduled and Non-Scheduled languages. The former is a set of 18 languages that appear in the VIIIth Schedule of the Indian Constitution, thus the term 'Scheduled Languages'. Only these 18 languages receive funding from the Central government in New Delhi for language maintenance, which include making provisions for these languages to be taught in the national school system as media of instruction, second or third languages. Linguistic groups must mobilize themselves to attain the privileged status of entering their languages as Scheduled Languages. The linguistic history of India, since the country gained independence from the British in 1947, shows that through political movements, some of which resulted in constitutional amendments, many new languages have been added to the VIIIth Schedule. According to the 1991 census, 18 languages are considered Scheduled Languages (Table 1.2, Bose, 1998: 151).

In December 2003 four minority languages, Bodo, Dogri, Maithili and Santali, were added to the list of Scheduled languages, bringing the total up to 22. This was implemented when the Parliament of India passed the Constitutional Bill of 2003, which is the 100th amendment to the Constitution of India (Mohanty, 2006).

The list of Non-Scheduled Languages consists of 96 dialects or languages, as shown in Appendix 1. As this list is from the 1991 census, it also includes Bodo, Dogri, Maithili and Santali, which, as mentioned in the previous paragraph, are now in the list of Scheduled Languages. Though the strength of some Non-Scheduled languages, like Bhili/Bhilodi spoken by 5,572,308, is more than that of Konkani (no. 15 in Table 1.2),

Table 1.2 Scheduled languages and percentage of speakers (1991 census)

Number	Languages	Percentage of mother tongue speakers
1	Hindi	39.85
2	Bengali	8.22
3	Telugu	7.80
4	Marathi	7.38
5	Tamil	6.26
6	Urdu	5.13
7	Gujarati	4.81
8	Kannada	3.87
9	Malayalam	3.59
10	Oriya	3.32
11	Punjabi	2.76
12	Assamese	1.55
13	Sindhi	0.25
14	Nepali	0.25
15	Konkani	0.21
16	Manipuri	0.15
17	Kashmiri	[a]
18	Sanskrit	0.01

[a] Bose comments here that the number of Kashmiri speakers is not valid due to political instability in the state

a Scheduled language spoken only by 1,760,607, Non-Scheduled languages do not have funding from the Central Government. In fact, most Non-Scheduled languages are spoken by tribal communities in the Central or North-Eastern States of India. In the context of India 'tribal' refers to communities, usually of non-Aryan origin, which some anthropologists consider to be the indigenous inhabitants of the Indian subcontinent predating the Aryans. These are disadvantaged groups living in remote rural areas practicing a highly animistic form of religion that some think is a form of Hinduism. Tribal communities are one of the least mobilized in the country. However, there is a Commissioner of Linguistic Minorities to protect their rights. The VIIIth Schedule is a highly amended document: as groups mobilize themselves and agitate for linguistic human rights, new languages are added to it. Of the 18 languages shown in Table 1.2, only 15 existed in the original set made in 1956.

National language policy and schooling

India's national language policy, which was formulated in the 1950s, is modeled on that of the then USSR, a gigantic influence on the socialist politics and economy of India until the 1990s. The status of national language that Russian occupied in the language planning of the ex-Soviet Union was given to Hindi by language planners in India. Like Russian, Hindi has uneasily worn this crown. In the Indian Constitution of 1950 Hindi was declared the national language and English the official language for the next 15 years till 1965. In these 15 years there was meant to be adequate corpus planning in Hindi to equip it to take over the role of official language from English. However, as 1965 approached there were linguistic riots in the southern state of Tamil Nadu, as non-Hindi speakers sensed impending disenfranchisement. In the face of such opposition, Jawaharlal Nehru, then Prime Minister of India, had the Constitution amended and in 1968 both Hindi and English were declared co-official languages. Though corpus planning in Hindi still continues, there is no date on which it is supposed to take over from English as an official language, a strategy of ambiguity that has successfully created the illusion of equitable distribution of linguistic capital.

Currently both Hindi and English are co-official languages. The Constitution of India does not contain a statement that declares Hindi to be the national language of the country. Each of the 28 states within the Indian federation has its own 'national' and official language combinations. These states were established in 1956 along linguistic boundaries, i.e. Hindi-speaking people were grouped into the state of Uttar Pradesh, Marathi speakers into Maharashtra and so on. Thus the geographical boundary of each Indian state is actually an isogloss. This linguistic organization of states, which was opposed unsuccessfully by both Gandhi and Nehru, was the result of mini nationalisms that in India have always centered around language as providing a distinct group identity.

Providing free and compulsory basic education till the age of 14 for all Indian citizens, a constitutional right, is a serious challenge for a developing country with a population of one billion. Though the Central Government has made strides, basic education is still a privilege, not a right. Table 1.3

Table 1.3 Growth of recognized educational institutions

Years	Primary	Upper primary	Secondary	Colleges for general education	Colleges for professional education (engineering, medicine etc.)	Univer-sities
1950–51	209,671	13,596	7416	370	208	27
2001–02	664,041	219,626	133,492	8737	2409	272

Source: Department of Education, Government of India; http:/education.nic.in

is a snapshot of the growth of the school infrastructure in India. The educational institutions represented in Table 1.3 are managed by government bodies and do not include a large number of elite educational institutions that are privately funded. However, a majority of Indians use the subsidized government school system. The most widespread amongst these are the Kendriya Vidyalayas (Central Schools), supplemented by chains like the Rajkiya Sarvodaya Kanya Vidyalayas (Sarvodaya Girls Schools) and Nagar Nigam Bal Vidyalayas (Municipal Schools). All schools in India, private and government funded, have to implement the TLF.

Though India has worked towards improving educational statistics, a lot more needs to be done. According to the 2001 census the literacy rate of India is 65.38% and that of the city of Delhi 81.82%. In both statistics great strides have been made since the 1991 census, which showed the literacy rate in India to be 51.63%, and that of Delhi as only 75.29% (www.censusindia.net). However, I also agree with Dreze and Sen that in the field of elementary education India has done worse than even the average of the poorest countries of the world. In this respect India is behind Ghana, Indonesia, Kenya, Burma, Philippines, Zimbabwe and Zambia (Dreze & Sen, 2005).

Vernaculars as media of instruction

In a multilingual country like India, media of instruction has always been a highly contested linguistic site. In 1882 there was a raging debate amongst the intelligentsia and the masses about media of instruction in the national school system. For instance the Sikh National Association wrote a memorandum to the Education Commission asking for Punjabi-medium education in primary schools in Punjab instead of Urdu-medium education, which was current at that time. In the same year the Punjab Brahma Samaj put in their petition for Persian and Urdu in the primary schools of Punjab to be replaced by Hindi. The arguments of these social groups were that Urdu is a foreign language for Hindus who speak Hindi in the province of Punjab. The replacement of Urdu by Hindi was contested by Muslims in the districts of Aligarh, Bulandshahr, Rurki and Meerut, who filed a petition of their own with the Education Commission. In this document they asserted that, 'Urdu is not our religious or national language. Nor was it introduced here from any foreign country. It is the product of India itself. It owes its origin to the joint action of both the Hindus and the Muhammedans. It has thus gradually become the vernacular language of India' (Bhattacharya *et al.*, 2003: 173). Similarly the priestly class of Hindus wanted Sanskrit to have a place in the education system and some religious education to be built into the curriculum.

These debates confronted the Indian National Congress in 1947 when India became independent. Meeting the demands of the major linguistic groups and at the same time forging a national character through a common language was a serious challenge for a young nation. This was dealt with by the TLF.

The Three Language Formula

India's language-in-education policy, the TLF, was recommended by the All India Council for Education in 1956. It is part of the Kothari Commission Report of 1964–65, which is a comprehensive document planning India's educational future. After various modifications the TLF was codified in the National Policy on Education in 1968, which is considered by most sociolinguists as the date when the TLF came into effect. This language in education policy was endorsed by the National Education Policy of 1986 and then again by the Programme of Action in 1992, testifying not only to the entrenched nature of the TLF but also to the sensitivity of language issues in India, which the government thinks is best left untouched (Annamalai, 2001). In addition to being India's bilingual education policy in the national school system, it is also part of the state's agenda for promoting multilingualism/multiculturalism and equipping Indians with a language of globalization.

According to the TLF all school-going children will have first, second and third languages by the time they complete secondary school. The first language or medium of instruction is the mother tongue/regional standard language, which must be used at the primary school stage (Grades 1–5). In cases where children speak a dialect of the regional standard or a different language altogether, they are being educated in a language different from their mother tongue. The second and third languages are introduced in secondary school (Grades 6–10, divided into lower and higher secondary) and are:

(1) Modern Indian Language (MIL) for Hindi speaking children, Hindi for non-Hindi speakers.
(2) English.

In many cases a classical Indian language like Sanskrit is taught to Hindi speakers instead of a modern Indian language.

The TLF is customized in each of the 28 states that make up the Indian federation. For instance the teaching of Hindi is obligatory in all Indian states except in Tamil Nadu, Tripura and the Karaikal region of Pondicherry. Similarly, though the teaching of English is obligatory, the state of Bihar refuses to comply. The state of West Bengal refuses to teach Hindi. The stage at which the second and third languages are introduced is dependent on the resources and ideology of the state. In general English is compulsorily taught in Grades 6–9.

Despite the entrenched nature of the TLF, it has numerous draw-backs. Annamalai (2001) raises the issue that the TLF does not really contribute to multilingualism in India. He writes that multilingualism in India is of three types: formal, nonformal and informal. The first is implemented through schooling, the second through adult literacy programs, distance learning and other such programs, and finally informal multilingualism is created through the lived experience of an Indian. Though the census data that Annamalai uses, from 1961 and 1981, are dated considering the year the book was published, he shows convincingly that 'in the bilingualism of the school age group less than half is contributed by schooling' (Annamalai, 2001: 52). The 1991 census shows that .19.44% of India's population is bilingual and 7.26% trilingual (http://www.censusindia.net/results/provindia3.html). Though these numbers look somewhat strange to me because I have never really met an Indian who is truly monolingual, I share Annamalai's hypothesis that this is the result not of schooling but mainly of 'informal' learning of languages that takes place in the life of an Indian.

A further shortcoming of the TLF is that it does not accommodate languages that are not regional standard languages, thus giving primacy to the needs of the state rather than the individual. For instance very few of the languages and dialects in Appendix 1 are part of the TLF, as they are the languages of disenfranchised, mainly tribal, minorities. Thus the TLF is not able to make good the Constitutional directive that the medium of education in primary school must be the mother tongue. Also, there is no constitutional or legal definition of a Modern Indian Language (MIL).

In most schools MILs are not taught to Hindi speakers; instead a classical language like Sanskrit or Arabic is taught. Finally it favors Hindi speakers by laying less of a burden on them for acquiring a third language as compared to non-Hindi speakers.

The main strength of the TLF is that it has created English-knowing bilinguals, as English is learned, especially by disadvantaged groups, mainly through formal schooling. The TLF then is an egalitarian language in education policy that, unlike the English language policy instituted by Thomas Babington Macaulay in 1835, is a policy of decolonization and equitable access to linguistic capital (Vaish, 2004). This is not the forum where I can describe in detail the way English language policy was used to exploit colonial India. The point to note is that the current language in education policy is implemented through the national school system that offers low cost sustainable education to the majority. As such English in the TLF is disseminated in an egalitarian manner, unlike in colonial India, where English was supplied to only the elite to hegemonize them. The nonformal sector outside the national school system also provides access to English through courses, for instance the 'Rapidex English Speaking Course', which is advertised all over Delhi. Though these courses are expensive, the disadvantaged try to take them to supplement the English they have been taught in school.

Hybridity: The Politics of Hindi

I see hybridity as syncretism in language use: hybridity is to literary criticism what codeswitching is to sociolinguistics. It includes the way speakers codeswitch, mix and borrow between, for instance, Hindi and English and 'do identity' through such language use. There is also the idea of hybridity in language in society, which refers to the way languages reinvent and transmogrify themselves in response to the political and personal conditions of the lived experience of speakers rather than the language planning of institutionalized agencies. In the case of Hindi and its spoken code Hindustani, the idea of hybridity refers to a syncretic language that celebrates the plurilingual nature of Indian identity, in opposition to purist language planning trends that, for instance, create separate identities for Hindi-speaking Hindus and Urdu-speaking Muslims.

The politics of language planning in Hindi show centripetal and centrifugal forces. On the one hand is the syncretic informal linguistics propagated by Mohandas Karamchand Gandhi that he inherited from traditions like Sufism. These I see as centrifugal forces that move away from the center and try to include an expanding group of speakers into its fold. On the other hand is the caste-based Sanskritized language planning of purists. These are centripetal forces that try to push the isogloss of a language towards the centre in an attempt to condense the group within a shrinking boundary, a sociolinguistic phenomenon that most likely results in loss of ethnolinguistic vitality, language shift and loss of speakers.

Gandhi's Hindi

Nandy (1983; 1995) suggests that the ideas of Mohandas Karamchand Gandhi, whether they had to do with politics, language or religion, were based on a fundamental principle of cohesion in the immense diversity of India. Like a master showman in front of huge crowds, Gandhi would mix cultures, castes, languages and religions, which was the basis of his popularity. It is because of this hybridity that Gandhi, even though he never ran for office, or held a formal political position, as his place in Indian politics was always symbolic, was able to draw crowds the way other Indian politicians, like Jawarharlal Nehru, found impossible.

Apparently Gandhi once remarked that it cost the British Government a lot to keep him in poverty. Whether this was true or not Gandhi was, indeed, the ultimate subaltern. He owned nothing, spun the meager cloth on his small wiry body, and held no formal political office. His gigantic moral stature, he is considered the father of the Indian nation, was entirely based on how he represented his subalternity and ultimately it was this moral stature that convinced the British to withdraw from India. Nowhere else in the world was colonialism shamed into retreat as it was in India by the person Winston Churchill called 'the half naked fakir'.

Young (2001) extends Nandy's ideas on Gandhi into linguistics through his analysis of the way Gandhi used समस (Samas) and सन्धी (Sandhi). Both these are linguistic principles in Sanskrit which have to do with the coining of new words. In Samas two antithetical words can be conjoined as in सुखदुख 'sukhdukh' (happiness/sadness). In Sandhi the principle is the same except that the new word will undergo some modification. For instance the word for signature in Hindi is a sandhi between हस्त which means hand and अक्षर which means letter. Together these two words make हस्ताक्षर, meaning signature. Using these linguistic principles to create a Hindustani that would include all the languages of India was what Gandhi had dreamed would be the national language of India.

Gandhi's fundamental contribution to language in India is the idea of हिन्दुस्तानी. The word is actually a mixture of two words, हिन्दु (*Hindu*) and स्तान (*Stan*). The first refers to the religion by the same name and the second is Urdu for 'place of'. Thus हिन्दुस्तान is Urdu for 'the land of the Hindu' and, by extension, हिन्दुस्तानी (*Hindustani*) is the language of the people. By hybridizing an Urdu word into the language of India Gandhi was deliberately trying to include the Muslim and other minority groups into what he hoped would become a syncretic national language. In the following section I explore the reasons why this hybrid Hindustani did not become officialized and in fact English became more of a link language between Indians of different linguistic groups instead of Hindustani.

Agnihotri (2007) documents the debates in the Constituent Assembly set up in 1946 with over 300 members. Among the issues debated in the Constituent Assembly were the linguistic division of the states in India, what the national and official languages would be and in what scripts these would be written. Specifically Agnihotri analyzes the debate regarding the acceptance of Hindustani as the national and official language of India. Despite the fact that heavyweights in the Indian National Congress like Jawaharlal Nehru and Mohandas Karamchand Gandhi were for the adoption of Hindustani, the Hindi lobby won this debate by, exactly, one vote.

The problem with officializing Hindi

The Indian National Congress decided that from the date of the Indian Constitution (1950), for the next 15 years, English would be used as an official language and Hindi would undergo corpus planning so that it could displace English in 1965 as the official language. Schiffman (1996) rightly comments that this language policy was heavily influenced by that of the ex-Soviet Union, as at that time many of the Indian leaders had socialist leanings. He writes:

> The 1950 policy was without doubt a clone of the Soviet model developed and implemented by Lenin in the USSR in the 1920s (and by Stalin in the 1930s), with the role occupied by Russian in that policy tailored for Hindi in India's policy. More or less slavish imitation of this policy, I claim, has led to incongruities that have plagued the policy from its inception to this day, and are now quiescent only because of the stalemate arrived at in Shastri's 'Three-Language Formula' of 1964–5. (Schiffman, 1996: 150)

The decision to base India's language policy on that of the ex-Soviet Union was founded on the report of S.G. Barve, who traveled to the Soviet Union to observe the conditions there and make recommendations to Indian politicians. Schiffman (1996: 163) quotes a comment by Barve that was ultimately disregarded by Indian politicians and that has led to many of the language problems we have today:

> In a sense, the Indian problem is not similar to but sharply contrasted to the Russian [i.e. Soviet model]. In Russia they had a historical tradition as well as the elements of a situation in which a strong pan-Russian medium of expression was readily available; their undertaking was the comparatively easier, congenial and 'flattering' task of developing and 'enfranchising' local languages that had been suppressed under the weight of too great an insistence on the common linguistic medium. In Indian conditions the problem is that we have strong regional languages and we have to evolve anew a linguistic medium for pan-Indian purposes out of the regional language spoken by the most numerous linguistic group in the country.

However this advice was not heeded and as 1965 approached there were rumblings of discontent, particularly in the southern state of Tamil Nadu where there were riots and self-immolations. Thus the Official Languages Act was passed in 1963 (amended in 1967), which allowed the use of English as a co-official language indefinitely. 'The Act also lays down that both Hindi and English shall compulsorily be used for certain specified purposes, such as resolutions, general orders, rules, notifications, press communiqués, administrative and other reports, licences, permits, contracts, agreements, etc.' (Ministry of Information and Broadcasting, 2000: 40). In addition it ensured that Hindi could be used in communication between the Central Government in New Delhi and Hindi-speaking states, and English between the Centre and non-Hindi-speaking states (Brass, 1990: 144–145).

In the interim various linguistic commissions were set up to modernize Hindi so that it could meet the requirements of an official language, and their work constitutes corpus planning in Hindi. In 1950 the Ministry of Education sponsored the Board of Scientific Terminology 'which was assigned the job of preparing 350,000 new terms in Hindi, of which 290,000 were produced by 1963' (DasGupta, 1970: 165). Today this board exists as the Commission for Scientific and Technical Terminology. Similarly the Kendriya Hindi Samiti (Central Hindi Committee) and the Hindi Salahakar Samiti (Hindi Advisory Committee) help to propagate and develop Hindi, reviewing the progress made in Hindi as an official language in various government ministries, and submit reports. The Department of Official Language publishes Rajbhasha Bharti (India's language), manuals, posters and calendars depicting the use of Hindi in various spheres. There is a

Central Translation Bureau to translate manuals, codes and nonstatutory literature for government offices and banks, from English to Hindi and vice versa (Ministry of Information and Broadcasting, 2000).

DasGupta (1977) argues that corpus planning in Hindi is a top-down process. There are three main government bodies involved in the development of Hindi:

(1) The Central Hindi Directorate and the Commission for Scientific and Technical Terminology (in the Ministry of Education, now called Ministry of Human Resource Development).
(2) Official Language Commission (in the Ministry of Law).
(3) Hindi Training Scheme (in the Home Ministry).

In interviewing officials in these organizations DasGupta (1977: 59) found that their top-level goal was 'increased lexical stock and energetic dissemination and use'. He found that very few of the personnel in these outfits were linguists or educationists. Most of them were bureaucrats drawn from the Indian Civil Services. Each of these units was a bureaucracy and not at all an academy. These organizations had very little contact with writers and journalists, the broadcasting world or with language planning organizations in other countries. Also 'the agencies put a high premium on quantity of output and give less attention to quality, user acceptance and public reaction' (DasGupta, 1977: 77). Thus the demand for corpus planning comes as a top-down order from higher government offices and not from the public. DasGupta argues that because implementation is a top-down approach it is not accepted by the public and one never hears these new Hindi words being used in the country. In fact both the people educated in the vernaculars and illiterate people use English words for public institutions or other scientific terms.

Like DasGupta (1977), Aggarwal (2000: 139) is correct in noting that 'Despite all the provisions and policy statements, Hindi or any other Indian language has not yet been raised, in practice, to the position of the most popularly used language in administration, judiciary, business, industry and information technology, science and technology'. Aggarwal goes on to say that English has overtaken Hindi in all these fields and even the rural first-generation learners aspire to a working knowledge of English.

Caste-based language planning

The kind of corpus planning that has been taking place in Hindi has political implications, in that it favors the higher castes or classes of Hindi speakers. The committees involved in the corpus planning of Hindi borrowed generously from Sanskrit. In this way they moved Hindi away from 'Hindustani' where there is an amalgam of Hindi and Urdu. At the time of independence Gandhi wanted Hindustani and not pure Hindi to be the national language of the country. Had this been accepted the Muslim minority would have been appeased. However, corpus planning, which was based only on Sanskrit, and which I would like to call caste-based corpus planning, gave Hindi a very Hindu nature and alienated the Urdu-speaking Muslim community. Pattanayak (1986: 30) writes that the 'spread of Hindi was interpreted as Hinduization rather than Indianization'. This Sanskritized corpus planning ensured that the Muslims would not accept Hindi as their national language.

Also, Hindi failed to gain vitality among the Hindi speakers themselves, who preferred to use the English term for a technical word. Thus Pattanayak (1986: 29) finds that 'Hindi did not even become an effective instrument of daily life in the Hindi zone itself'. Schiffman (1996) confirms this and asserts that language planners in India have not heeded the fact that Indian languages tend to diglossify themselves and no interest is shown in the L variety, which is what everyone is speaking. On the other hand 'True to the tradition of the traditional Indian literati, they are developing Hindi in a direction that tends to make the new Hindi a compartmentalized preserve of the Hindi literary elite' (Schiffman, 1996: 167).

Srivastava (1979) shows why Hindi was not accepted as an official language by the south even though the south is largely Hindu. From 12–14 September 1949, there was a raging debate in the Constituent Assembly on the national/official language issue between the pro- and anti-Hindi blocs. The result of this debate were articles 120(1) and 343–351 in the Indian Constitution of 1950, which deal with the official language issue, the relevant portions of which are quoted below:

343. Official language of the Union

(1): The official language of the Union shall be Hindi in Devanagari Script. The form of numerals to be used for the official purposes of the Union shall be the international form of Indian numerals.

(2): Notwithstanding anything in the clause (1), for a period of fifteen years from the commencement of the constitution the English language shall continue to be used for all the official purposes of the Union for which it was being used immediately before such commencement: provided that the President may during the said period, by order 306 authorize the use of the Hindi language in addition to the English language and of the Devanagari form of numerals in addition to the international form of Indian numerals for any of the official purposes of the Union.

(3): Notwithstanding anything in this article, Parliament may by law provide for the use, after the said period of fifteen years, of –

the English language, or

the Devanagari form of numerals, for such purposes as may be specified in the law. (http://www.constitution.org/cons/india)

Thus the framers of India's Constitution in 1950 made sure that they included clause 3, which allowed the country to add English as an additional or co-official language. Clearly in 1950 there were concerns about whether 15 years later Hindi, despite all the corpus planning, would be able to become a pan-Indian language. At the same time there is ambiguity in the very article that proposes how Hindi can become a pan-Indian language:

351:

It shall be the duty of the Union to promote the spread of the Hindi language, to develop it so that it may serve as a medium of expression for all the elements of the composite culture of India and to secure its enrichment by assimilating without interfering with its genius, the form, style and expressions used in Hindustani and in the other languages of India specified in the VIIIth Schedule, and by drawing, wherever necessary or desirable, for its vocabulary, primarily on Sanskrit and secondarily on other languages. (http://www.constitution.org/cons/india)

Though Article 351 recommended that development in Hindi should represent the composite culture of India, it recommends that this be done by drawing vocabulary 'primarily from Sanskrit and secondarily on other languages'. In interpreting this clause corpus planners have laid more emphasis on this part of the sentence than on the idea of creating a 'composite culture of India' by drawing on Hindustani.

Caste-based language planning in Hindi disenfranchised the people of south India who felt that if government jobs require knowledge of Hindi they would be excluded from one of the main sources of employment. This political agenda was taken up by the Dravida Munnetra Kazhagam (DMK), a leading political party in south India in opposition to the Congress party, which also supported the development of the Tamil language. The DMK's agitation was also against the upper-caste Brahmins and what it thought was an Aryanization of India through the domination of lower castes who did not know Sanskrit.

As 1965, the year that Hindi was supposed to displace English as an official language, approached, the DMK intensified its agitation against Hindi. It organized the Madras state anti-Hindi conference on 17 January 1965. 26 January of the same year, which is India's independence day, was declared a day of mourning. On this day, amidst numerous agitations and processions, two workers from the DMK immolated themselves and about 70 people were killed in police encounters. In the face of such strong opposition, Nehru, then Prime Minister of India, ordered the Official Language Amendment Act of 1967. This Act stated:

> Notwithstanding the expiration of the period of 15 years from the commencement of the Constitution, the English language may, as from the appointed day, continue to be used, in addition to Hindi (a) for all the official purposes of the Union for which it was being used immediately before that day: and (b) for the transaction of business in Parliament. (http://www.constitution.org/cons/india)

Thus officialization of Hindi was problematic for the Urdu-speaking Muslim minority, for the south Indians who are Hindus and to some extent for Hindi speakers themselves, in that they have not been able to internalize the new Sanskrit-based lexicon and prefer to use the English word instead. This problematization of language policy regarding Hindi also shows how volatile language issues are in India and how inextricably they are linked with caste, religion and employment opportunities. India is probably one of the few countries in the world where people immolate themselves publicly on language issues. It is with this linguistic landscape in mind that we now turn to the positionality of English.

Positionality of English

The term 'positionality' in postcolonial theory signifies the power-politics inherent in the status of a phenomenon. As such it differs from the word 'position', which is neutral and apolitical. A few Indian scholars think that Hindi is losing a power struggle with English. For instance Dua (1996), a strong supporter of Hindi, blames defective language planning policies for the current perceived defeat that Hindi is suffering against the onslaught of English. He has an even bleaker view of education in

India: 'No radical changes have taken place in the educational system since independence' because firstly the colonial system of education has not changed, secondly India's language planning and policy is marked by 'indecision, lack of vision, and inadequate understanding of ... education planning', and finally because the hegemony of English continues to support only the middle classes.

This bleak view feeds into preconceived notions that many Western scholars, like Phillipson (1992), have of language policies in developing countries and does great disservice to the exciting educational changes that are taking place in India at the grassroots. Though there is no doubt that language planning in Hindi has not been stellar, it is still spoken by nearly 40% of one billion people and there is no indication that Hindi is being left behind by English in the race for linguistic survival. Census results for the past two decades show that there has been no decline in the number of Hindi speakers. For instance the number of speakers for Hindi from the 1981 census shows that at that time Hindi was spoken by 39.94% of the country (Mahapatra, 1990), which is comparable to the number of speakers in 1991 – 39.65%. Also, in Vaish (2005) I have shown that the idea that English is a killer language that endangers local languages and cultures is a kind of postcolonial Orientalism not applicable to India. Here suffice it to say that the positionality of English in Indian multilingualism is that it adds a workplace literacy, a new social field in the Bourdieu-sian sense, to the repertoire of a bi/multilingual individual. The habitus of postcolonial India has internal forces of resistance that do not allow English to be a killer language.

English is empowering in postcolonial India because of its positionality vis-à-vis the indigenous languages in the TLF. Knowledge of English is like a vocational skill that a subaltern invests in to get a better job while the social fields of religion, culture, family and friends are sustained by the mother tongue. In this sociolinguistic matrix there is an inherent ecological balance that does not endanger the biodiversity of languages in India with the threat of language loss and shift. The following brief case study of Ram Nivas and his language attitudes introduces the idea of how languages in India tend to be maintained in an ecological balance.

Ram Nivas: A case study of subaltern speak

I first met Ram Nivas in December 1999 when I started my data collection in New Delhi. The reason I needed him was that negotiating traffic in Delhi requires nerves of steel, which I seemed to have left behind in the USA, where I was living at that time, and thus I needed a competent driver. He has neatly oiled hair, a shiny healthy complexion and comes to

work formally dressed in a clean, ironed shirt, pants, and socks and shoes.
When I go to the car to meet him he is usually reading a religious book in
Hindi. When I asked him if he liked reading other materials like novels
he remarked:

> Madam, मैं meat नहीं खाता, शराब नहीं पीता और novel नहीं पढ़ता ।
> Madam, I don't eat meat, drink alcohol or read novels.

During the course of driving me around Ram Nivas became, and still is,
one of my key informants and, in fact, friends.

He was born in 1965 in Paabi village, which is on the outskirts of Delhi.
His mother died when he was a child and he doesn't even remember her
face. He was brought up by Daadi (paternal grandmother). After primary
school he went for 'inter' to Lodi, a neighboring town, as Paabi did not
have any secondary or high schools in Ram Nivas' time. In 'inter' he
studied English and Sanskrit as second languages, both of which he found
tough. When he finished inter, which is equivalent to class 12, one 'babu'
(this term refers to someone who is English educated and from the middle
class) asked if he could drive and got him a job as a driver. Currently Ram
Nivas is a driver for the State Government of Delhi.

Ram Nivas has six children and all but one, who did not get admission, as
the admissions are by lottery, are in a Rajkiya Sarvodaya Vidyalaya, though
not in the branch where I have been conducting participant observations.
The one who got left behind in the lottery is in a Municipal Corporation
of Delhi school where English is taught only as a second language and is
not offered as a medium of instruction. Of the five children in the Rajkiya
Sarvodaya Vidyalayas, only one, Priyanka Kumari, was not able to get
into the English-medium stream, as there was no seat available when she
was being admitted. Thus Priyanka is in the Hindi medium of her school.
All four children in the English medium in the Rajkiya Sarvodaya Vidyalaya near his home are doing well. The oldest, Sandeep Kumar (b. 1988), is
good in science. The next, Dinesh Singh (b. 1990), wants to join the army.
Ghanshyam Kumar and Shashibala (b. 1995), the twins, are in Grade 4 and
it's too early to tell what they would like to be when they grow up.

When I asked Ram Nivas why he moved to Delhi he said:

> इन्ही के भविष्य के लिए । मैं तो जो बनना था बन गया । इनमे से कोई निकल जाए
> तो इनके पीछे मैं लगा हूँ । यदि यह पढ़ाई गाँव में मिलती तो मैं नहीं आता । खैर
> पढ़ाते तो यहाँ भी नहीं हैं पर यहाँ tuition वगैरह लगा कर बच्चा होशियार हो जाता
> है । वहाँ नहीं होता । वहाँ tuition भी नहीं लग पाता । English का नाम सुनते
> ही कांपने लग जाएंगे । 4th class की किताब नहीं पढ़ पाते inter वाले ।... शुरु से
> मिली नहीं उनको ।

For their future. I have become what I had to become. Amongst them if even one can get out of our social class into a higher class, so I'm working very hard with them. If this education was available in the village I would not have come. Anyway, even here they don't teach but with tuition etc. the child becomes smart. Not there. There tuition is also not available. They tremble the moment they hear the name of the English language. Those in 'inter' cannot read 4th grade books. They did not get English from the beginning. (20 March 2005)

Ram Nivas is very ambitious for his children. Not only did he move to Delhi for a better education, he moved mainly for access to the English language. He says that people in the village tremble at the English language because they have not studied it from the beginning like his children have. Even those who do learn English in the village learn very little and a student in high school or 'inter' is not able to read the text of a child in Grade 4 in Delhi. Sandeep enjoys science, which is in English, and Ram Nivas hopes he will be a doctor.

Ram Nivas is extremely aware of English as linguistic capital that can be converted to economic capital. He says that this is the language in which various exams can be taken to enter upper-class professions like the Indian Administrative Service (IAS). He informed me that this exam could only be taken in English until as late as 1989–90. At that time there was a major agitation by a group of activists who demanded that they be allowed to take this exam in Hindi. After at least three years of agitation now the IAS exam can be taken in Hindi but there is still one paper in English (field notes 20 March 2005). Ram Nivas is also aware of English as a language of computers. He says:

> जो आजकल computer का रिवाज़ चल रहा है वो सब English में है । नौकरी भी जाओ तो हिन्दी मे कोई कराता नहीं ।

> These days the trend for computers is all in English. If you go for a job, they do not do it in Hindi. (20 March 2005)

In aspiring for his children to take the IAS exam or join the computer industry, Ram Nivas is clearly positioning the English language as a tool with which he can break the constraints of class and caste. His comment on the IAS exam being only in English is indicative of the gatekeeping that the Indian upper classes had been maintaining through English. As a driver for the State Government of India, Ram Nivas' job is to ferry IAS officers around the city. He listens to the conversations of the bureaucrats sitting in the passenger seats behind him and hopes that one day one of his children will be in that seat. His son can now take this exam in Hindi but there is still one paper that he will have to take in English, for which Ram Nivas is preparing him well.

Ram Nivas' instrumental attitude towards language makes him feel that Sanskrit is not worth spending too much time on. His children, apart from Hindi and English, are studying Sanskrit as part of the TLF. Though Ram Nivas is a practicing Hindu, his attitude to Sanskrit is not influenced by his religion. He remarks:

> संस्कृत तो हमारी वेदिक भाषा हो गई ना । तो वेद तो कोई पढ़ना नहीं चाहता । हर आदमी का यही है कि मेरा बच्चा अब English सीखे । क्योंकि संस्कृत में जाएगा तो ज्यादा से ज्यादा पंडित बन जाएगा । फिर पूजा पाठ कराएगा । और English मे तो वह computer भी सीख लेगा, IAS का exam भी दे देगा, कुछ भी बन जाएगा । Pilot बन जाएगा, या engineer बन जाएगा, या doctor बन जाएगा । बाकि वह संस्कृत उसमे help नहीं करती । ना उनका paper होता है संस्कृत मे ।

> Sanskrit is our Vedic language. So no one wants to study the Vedas. Each man wants his child to learn English. Because if he goes into Sanskrit, at most he will become a Pandit. Then he will conduct prayers. And through English he can learn computers, take the IAS exam, he can become anything. He can become a pilot, or engineer or doctor. Also, Sanskrit does not help in this. There are no exams (professional vocational) in Sanskrit. (25 March 2005)

Despite being a practicing Hindu, and one who takes great interest in religious philosophy, Ram Nivas does not think Sanskrit has much currency. He thinks it is a waste of time because it can only get his son a Pandit's job, which does not pay well. However English has the power to change social class in one generation. Perhaps Ram Nivas' desire to convert linguistic into economic capital is extreme, but he is focused in his ambitions for his children and determined that they will not end up 'in the driver's seat' like him. He is aware of the drawbacks of the Rajkiya Sarvodaya Vidyalaya education, or government school education in general, and does remark that even in Delhi schools the quality of teaching leaves much to be desired. However, he has compensated for this with extensive daily tuition. Though this is a strain on his meager income of about Rs. 6000/ month (US$120), he has engaged a tutor for his children who comes every day and only has Sunday off.

Conclusions

This chapter has tried to trace the processes of decolonization in the realm of language and education in independent India. It has shown the linguistic diversity of India and the challenges that faced the Indian National Congress in formulating a national education policy when the country became independent in 1947. The positionality of English in postcolonial globalizing India is a tool of decolonization that is increasingly becoming accessible to subalterns on their own terms. The TLF has been successful, despite its drawbacks, as a language in education policy as it has accommodated the language loyalties of diverse ethnic groups. Finally, by repositioning English, a phenomenon that will be described in detail in the ensuing chapters, the TLF has reinvented itself to accommodate changes demanded by a globalizing economy.

This chapter has also analyzed the major language in society debates that are integral to the language situation in India. In particular it has analyzed the failure to establish Hindi as a national language due to contesting views from within the Hindi-speaking belt and from non-Hindi speakers who felt threatened by Hindi. The hybrid Hindustani that Gandhi wanted was not officialized in India though, ironically, this Hindustani is the language spoken by most Hindi speakers. It is a language in which there is codeswitching and -mixing from English and other Indian languages like Punjabi, Urdu and, in some domains, Sanskrit. Finally, Ram Nivas, a parent who has six children in two government schools in Delhi, has been introduced. Ram Nivas' instrumental attitudes towards language and his hopes and aspirations for his children show how English is perceived by the subaltern as a tool to break the reproductive cycle of social class.

Chapter 2
Biliteracy and Globalization

The confluence of biliteracy and globalization is somewhat uncharted water. What text types and practices does one find at the lifeworlds of this confluence and what implications do they have for the bilingual classroom? Who are the main players at this meeting place of texts (as in biliteracy) and processes (as in globalization): markets, the changing workplace, policymakers, teacher practitioners or finally the consumers and producers of languages? What does a biliterate text in our globalizing world look like both in and outside the classroom?

This chapter will define the key terms of this book, biliteracy and globalization, and explore some answers to the questions above in an attempt to set up a conceptual framework. It will also introduce to the reader how the following four chapters, which analyze data from the RSKV, are organized. Furthermore I will introduce the term 'Sarvodaya', coined by Mohandas Karamchand Gandhi (1869–1948), and show not only how this concept is the foundation on which the chain of RSKV schools have been founded, but also how Sarvodaya is linked to biliteracy and globalization.

Biliteracy and Related Terminology

Hornberger (2007) points out that in the 1970s the word 'biliteracy' carried connotations of fluency or mastery in the reading and writing of two or more languages. Her own definition of biliteracy is 'any and all instances in which communication occurs in two (or more) languages in or around writing' (Hornberger, 2003: 35). This inclusive definition includes varying levels of competencies, text types (traditional and multimodal), and verbal and symbolic communication. It thus encompasses biliteracy as exhibited in the lifeworld of the bilingual, and not as confined only to the classroom through school-related texts. Hornberger's definition of biliteracy is embedded in her model: the Continua of Biliteracy. This model is a way of analyzing what is taught (content of biliteracy), in which languages it is taught (media of biliteracy), where it is taught (contexts of biliteracy) and what is the outcome of the teaching (development of biliteracy). It is Hornberger's contention that the more access learners have to points on the continua, the fuller their biliterate development (see also Hornberger, 1990b). This contention is based on the three dimensionality of the model and the nestedness of its parts that allow a learner easy access to any and all parts given the appropriate pedagogy, curriculum and biliteracy event.

Related terms that have currency today are multimodal literacy (Kress, 2003), which is literacy based on the affordances of a web page, gesture, sound and other semiotic symbols including script, new literacies that one finds in cyberspace or workplace (Lankshear & Knobel, 2003) and finally multiliteracies (Cope & Kalantzis, 2000). None of these terms is about multiple languages and scripts as directly as is the term 'biliteracy', though all these terms are based on linguistic and cultural diversity. The term that comes closest in meaning to biliteracy is 'multilingual literacies', used by Martin-Jones and Jones (2000). Recently Pahl (2006) has edited a book that ethnographically links New Literacy Studies to multimodality in an age of globalization. However, the multimodality inherent in the diverse scripts and languages a bilingual commands is not the major focus of this otherwise excellent volume.

Globalization

The literature on globalization can be considered somewhat bounded by two massive trilogies: Wallerstein's (1974, 1980, 1989) *World Systems Analysis* and Castells' (1996/2000, 1997/2004, 1998/2000) *The Information Age*. Both sets of work are brilliant in their analyses of the ways the globe is networked into congeries of empires, corporations, communities and pan-national organizations. However, Wallerstein's Marxist perspective is now dated due to the demise of communism as an enduring political alternative. Though Castells' early writings are Marxist, his later work is more applicable to the world in which we live today. The shortcoming of his trilogy is that the work does not make India a major focus as it does China, thus excluding not only a globalizing country of 1 billion people but also one of the dominant cultures of our world.

Globalization has been defined somewhat differently by economists (Bhagwati, 2004), sociologists (Castells, 1996/2000, 1997/2004, 1998/2000) and anthropologists (Appadurai, 1996; 2000) but they all agree on the high level of connectivity in this phenomenon between nations, corporations and individuals. Pieterse, the cultural anthropologist, gives a definition that encompasses many of these views. He writes that globalization 'is an objective, empirical process of increasing economic and political connectivity, a subjective process unfolding in consciousness as the collective awareness of growing global interconnectedness, and a host of specific globalizing projects that seek to shape global conditions' (Pieterse, 2004: 16–17). As a phenomenon, Friedman (2005) points out that globalization is not new; in fact it is a process that started around 1492 and has manifested itself in three phases so far. In the first phase, 1492–1800, globalization was about imperial forces acquiring colonies by brute force; the second phase, 1800–2000, saw the rise of multinationals and the early version of the world wide web; and finally, since 2000, globalization has been about individuals participating in the global economy leading to what Friedman calls a 'flat world' or level playing field.

Problematizing Globalization

Globalization is lauded by some (Drucker, 1993; Reich, 1991) but is looked at extremely critically, especially, by environmentalists (Shiva, 2000/2004) and also by educationists, who see this process as propagating the inequities of neoliberalism (Stromquist, 2002). This book is not about taking sides for or against globalization; however, I do believe that 'globalization' has become the whipping boy of the ills in our new social order. Whether it is environmental degradation, language loss or shift, poverty or the poor quality of education in government-subsidized national school systems, globalization is cited as the cause of all these problems. However, many of the ills in today's world existed before the processes of globalization were unleashed and there are other social malaise that have nothing to do with it.

In the field of economics Bhagwati (2004) and Sen (2004) give a convincing defense of globalization from the point of view of a developing country. Sen suggests that globalization is neither Western nor a curse. He writes that in 1000 A.D. high technology like the use and invention of paper, the printing press and the magnetic compass were technologies prevalent in China and this knowledge moved from the East to Europe. Similarly the use of the decimal system, developed in India between the 2nd and 6th centuries, was picked up by Arab traders and thus was introduced to the West through the processes of globalization. Consequently, 'Europe would have been a lot poorer – economically, culturally, and scientifically – had it resisted the globalization of mathematics, science and technology at that time' (Sen, 2004: 17). Similarly resisting globalization can prove detrimental to developing countries. In fact 'it can … cause non-Western societies to shoot themselves in the foot – even in their precious cultural foot' (Sen, 2004: 17). According to Sen globalization is not the problem; the equitable distribution of its benefits is.

Bhagwati (2004), also a leading Indian economist, goes through the issues of poverty, democracy, culture and the monopoly of transnational corporations to give a reasoned defense of globalization. His book has a wealth of experience from his work with the Indian government and American academia. He finds that 'anti-globalization sentiments are more prevalent in the rich countries of the North, while pluralities of policy-makers and the public in the poor countries of the South see globalization instead as a positive force' (Bhagwati, 2004: 8). He makes a comparison between India and South East Asia to show how free trade, which is the key component of economic globalization, can alleviate poverty. From the 1960s to the 1980s India remained under the constraints of a socialist government whereas the 'four little tigers', Singapore, Hong Kong, South Korea and Taiwan, created the East Asian miracle by going from third to first world countries within a short span of about 30 years.

This book is not the place to go into all the main arguments of Bhagwati. The point I am trying to emphasize is what Bhagwati calls 'the tyranny of the missing alternative', referring to the dominance of theoretical and cultural perspectives that originate in the West. In this case it is the tyranny of the anti-globalization movement and the theorizing in the social sciences that stems from this movement According to Bhagwati this theorizing is not necessarily shared by the developing world, which tends to have a different, and in some cases far more positive, view of the processes of globalization. My theoretical perspective in this book shies away from the diatribe against globalization and presents a more balanced and, no doubt more positive, view of globalization from the point of view of a developing country.

In the field of sociology Castells' (all three volumes) monumental work gives an in-depth look at the nature of the new social order that is globalization. '...In a world submitted to cultural homogenization by the ideology of modernization and the power of global media, language, as the direct expression of culture, becomes the trench of cultural resistance, the last bastion of self-control, the refuge of identifiable meaning' (Castells, 2004: 56). This comment by Castells elaborates the central thesis in his three-volume work (Castells, 2000; 2000; 2004) that the new social order that has arisen in the era of globalization has created a tension between the Net and the Self. He traces the origins of this new social order from the 1970s in California when Silicon Valley was becoming the center for research and development in IT. This revolution in technology then spread to other parts of the world and today it is those countries that are not able to join the technology revolution, like third world countries in Africa and some Islamic nations, that are being left behind in the inexorable march of globalization.

The tension between the Net and the Self is also that between the global and local. In this tension there is a revival of local communities through 'urban social movements' for instance in American cities gangs have emerged as a major form of association work and identity for youth (Castells, 2004: 67). Thus Castells disagrees with Putnam's (1995) famous thesis of declining social capital in America based on poor attendance in various community organizations, religious groups and voting patterns. On the contrary Castells sees a revival of the local in reaction to the homogenizing forces of the global. Castells goes on to say that the Net creates a feeling of isolation and atomization in the individual which the local tries to overcome. '...People resist the process of individualization and social atomization, and tend to cluster in community organizations that, over time, generate a feeling of belonging, and ultimately, in many cases, a communal, cultural identity' (Castells, 2004: 64).

This tension between the Net and the Self is illustrated through the English language learning and work of bilinguals in India. In the unique linguistic ecology of India, diverse languages coexist without perceptible language loss; specifically the spread of global English has not caused language shift and loss of Indian languages. This affirmation of the Self through language and identity is illustrated in detail in Chapters 5 and 6 where I explore attitudes towards language and show how the 'agents' in a call center negotiate their fluctuating identities. The tension between the Net and the Self in India is manifested through instrumental attitudes towards English as the language of computers on the one hand and fierce linguistic and religious loyalty on the other. At the same time there are interstitial spaces of hybridity where, for instance, English is the language in which a student might decide to write a personal diary.

Outsourcing

Jyoti Kurrien: Call Centre worker

Jyoti, in her mid 30s, worked for Daksh e-services, which opened in 2000, for 2 1/2 years. She joined at the agent level and was promoted within 8 months to Senior Quality Specialist and finally Team Leader. Daksh is the largest call center in India. In 2004 it was bought by IBM and is now IBM-Daksh eServices managing the day to day correspondence of Amazon.com and one of the largest call center networks in the world.

As an agent Jyoti was given training in three main areas. The first week was soft skills like saying please, sorry and thank you and empathizing with the customer. Daksh does not train its agents in an American or British accent, emphasizing a global accent. The next two weeks was Voice and Linguistics where they were given training on voice modulation and grammar. The largest amount of time, six weeks, was spent on product related training. Though the attrition rate is high in call centers these are still prized jobs which pay about Rs. 15,000 to Rs. 20,000 (USD 300-500) per month. Also this attrition rate is much lower than in other parts of the world like the USA. Jyoti says that the quality of the recruits has changed. When she was working for Daksh the company hired personnel mainly from hotel management schools who already had some training in customer service. The people that are being hired now are often from government schools and might not have very good spoken English skills. They are trained on the job.

Jyoti left Daksh because she did not want a night job any more though she enjoyed her time in the call center. Her job began at 9p.m New Delhi time when it was 9a.m. in the US. She would come back home at about 10a.m and sleep the whole day which affected her personal life, especially her nascent marriage. However, she says that there are people for whom this salary will go a long way in providing for a family and since unemployment in India is high, there are many who value these jobs. In fact there were engineers, pilots and other professionals who were her colleagues as they could not find any other suitable jobs (field notes, March 30, 2005).

Jyoti's story is about outsourcing. One of the manifestations of economic globalization is the outsourcing of jobs from the first world to developing countries at tremendous savings for multinational corporations. For instance call centers employ 200,000 Indians at present and McKinsey predicts the ranks will swell to 1 million by 2008 (Sinha, 2003). The banking giant HSBC is moving 4000 jobs involving processing work and telephone enquiries to India, China and Malaysia. This move follows similar moves by British Telecom, Goldman Sachs, Abbey National and Prudential to outsource work to Asian economies to save costs (*The Straits Times*, 2003a: 7). This *Straits Times* article commented that 'In the past decade, India has emerged as a new hub for call centre operations because of its large number of well-educated, English speaking young people and low labor costs'. Outsourcing is an illustration of the globalization that Giddens (2001: 245) defines as a 'stretching process, in so far as the modes of connection between different social contexts or regions become networked across the earth's surface as a whole'.

According to a business story in the *International Herald Tribune* (Pollack, 2005: 15), 'The shifting of employment to countries like India and China that has occurred in manufacturing, back office work and computer programming is now spreading to a crown jewel of corporate America: the medical and drug sectors'. This article goes on to say that fueling the outsourcing trend are Indian and Chinese scientists who studied in the USA and Europe and are now going back to their countries with new business ideas. Forrester Research shows that of the 885,000 jobs in the life sciences sector in the USA, about 225,000 have moved offshore, mainly to Asia.

The loss of jobs in first world countries and the concomitant creation of employment in the developing world is a highly contested site. A *Business Week* issue that ran a cover story entitled 'The Rise of India: and what it means for the global economy' remarked 'India is at the center of a brewing storm in America…An outcry in Indiana recently prompted the state to cancel a \$15 million IT contract with India's Tata Consulting…Indiana notwithstanding, US governments are increasingly using India to manage everything from accounting to their food-stamp programs. Even the US Postal service is taking work there' (*Business Week*, 2003: 45). Despite this brewing storm, outsourcing to India is an inexorable juggernaut. In fact 'Global software orders to offshore centers like India are likely to rise by 30% annually in the next three years, according to a report last month based on joint studies by Bernstein Research and Everest Research Institute (Chatterjee & Somayaji, 2005: B1).

Not everyone in the developing world sees outsourcing as a golden opportunity for unemployed Indians. For instance, Sinha, in *Outlook*, a well known English weekly news magazine in India, reports:

> Recently, Harish Trivedi, English professor at Delhi University, wrote an angry rejoinder to an article published in the Times Literary Supplement that celebrated the success of Indians harvesting their English speaking skills through call centers. He dubbed the call centre customer jockeys, 'cyber coolies of our global age, working not on sugar plantations but on flickering screens, and lashed into submission through vigilant and punitive monitoring, each slip in accent or lapse in pretence meaning a cut in wages'. (Sinha, 2003: 56)

This rather extreme response does not do justice to either the reality on the ground or to the view of well respected Indian economists that I have discussed under the section on 'Problematizing Globalization'. No doubt globalization and outsourcing are highly contested aspects of our changing social order. My research sees the value of arguments raised by Sen and Bhagwati in the story of Jyoti Kurrien. As Jyoti's story reveals, there is a serious dearth of employment opportunities in India. As such this new employment sector absorbs many Indians who would otherwise find it difficult to support their families, providing them with access to sustainable labor, which is one of the foundations of 'Sarvodaya'.

The confluence of biliteracy and globalization

The themes that emerge from the field of biliteracy and globalization are changing media of instruction in national school systems, new literacies required in the workplace, the threatened linguistic ecology of the globe and finally biliterate textual practices influenced by the Internet. Each of these will be briefly described in this chapter, and in detail in the ensuing four chapters. Let me begin with changing media of instruction and new literacies. Block and Cameron (2002: 5) point out that 'globalization changes the conditions under which language learning takes place' by commodifying languages and creating new literacies required by the workplace that schools are expected to teach. This is definitely true of India. The Three Language Formula of India (TLF), described in detail in Chapter 1, which offered English as a second language only in secondary school, is being transformed by globalization. Because the urban disadvantaged are demanding earlier access to the linguistic capital of English, government schools find that offering English only in secondary school is too late and does not meet the demands of the community. This demand is linked to new sectors of the economy that are opening up since India started globalizing in 1991, like the mushrooming of call centers all over New Delhi. Consequently government schools have initiated dual medium programs which offer English as one of the media of instruction along with Hindi from nursery itself. The RSKV described in this book is one such school.

The spread of global English is perceived as threatening the linguistic diversity of the globe. Using the metaphor of biodiversity, Skutnabb-Kangas (2003) argues that not only can the world's linguistic diversity be documented in the same way as biodiversity, there is also a correlation, and even causal connection, between the two. She writes that 'Maintenance of diversities…is one end of the continuum where ecocide and linguistic genocide are at the other end' (Skutnabb-Kangas, 2003: 34). Skutnabb-Kangas' main point through these arguments is to raise awareness about language endangerment of small languages from the threat of big killer languages, like English. In a similar vein Phillipson (1992,

2006) sees globalization, Americanization and Englishization as parts of one process. He finds that English has retained its hold in former colonies and that it remains a divisive tool with which socioeconomic strata are separated into the haves and have-nots. In India, the argument that English is divisive, separating the haves from the have-nots, is supported by Ramanathan (2005).

This view has been critiqued by Canagarajah (1999), who shows how English has been appropriated in Sri Lanka, and Vaish (2005), who finds an agentive demand for and use of English in India. Vaish argues that in the cultural and linguistic terrain of India where language loyalty provides checks and balances to language loss and shift, the argument that the spread of English is linguistic racism does not hold true. Similarly Kumaravadivelu (2002) hypothesizes that if English is looked at from a postcolonial lens it looks like a divisive language of colonization. However, when looked at from the lens of globalization, it is a language of decolonization that students learn as a vocational skill to access the globalizing economy.

Contesting the well known view that globalization homogenizes languages is the not so well known literature documenting the rise of non-English languages due to globalization. Dor's (2004: 98) thesis is that 'the forces of globalization do not have a vested interest in the global spread of English. They have a short-term interest in penetrating local markets through local languages and a long-term interest in turning these languages into commodified tools of communication'. He predicts that the Internet 'is going to be a predominantly non-English-language medium'. In 2004 there were 280 million English users and no less than 657 million non-English users and this gap is widening in favor of the latter. A similar view is expressed by Indrajit Banerjee, secretary-general of the Asian Media Information and communication Centre (AMIC), who comments:

> One would think that globalization in Asia would mean going English but that's not the case...The diasporic market means you can have international newspapers, international TV and radio channels which are completely based on local languages. This is what I call the globalization of the local. (Soh, 2005: 29)

In keeping with Dor's view, Warschauer (2002) and Warschauer *et al.* (2002) point out that although English and Romanized languages are privileged in the Internet's history and design, this is changing due to the increasing online usage of languages like Arabic. For instance the website of CNNArabic. com is a biliterate text that uses both Roman and Arabic scripts. Interestingly it is also a multimodal text because it has photos, videos and sound. Also, in informal e-mails, colloquial Arabic is extensively used in the Roman script: a type of biliterate text that is becoming very common on the Internet.

I find a similar use of biliterate textual practices in data from India in communication between Hindi/English bilinguals. The following e-mail, which was sent to me by one of the young students in my study in India, is a case in point. Here the sender uses Romanized Hindi (bolded) and English to communicate.

Hi Mam

Main Bahut Khus Hua Apki E-Mail **Pakar**
(*I was very happy to receive your e-m*ail)

& Thanks for my reply.

Finally, English is not the only language to claim a global status. Goh (2000) stakes a similar claim for Mandarin, saying that like English it is used in inner, outer and expanding circles. Goh's claim is based on the increasing economic power of the inner circle (China) and the increasing number of Mandarin learners in the outer circle. Goh also points to the rising use of Mandarin on the Internet through sites like Chinese Google and Chinese Wikipedia. Thus the emergence of languages like Arabic and Mandarin in cyberspace and the mingling of scripts with diverse languages in informal communication point to new biliterate practices, which have yet to be explored in depth.

Similar Studies

Broadly speaking work in biliteracy tends to fall into two discrete domains: either the research is in the classroom or on the linguistic landscape of a site. A project of the former type is 'Signs of Difference: How Children Learn to Write in Different Script Systems', undertaken by the Institute of Education in the UK (Kenner, 2004; Kenner & Kress 2003). This was a year-long study of six-year-olds in London learning Chinese, Arabic and Spanish along with English. The methodology involved asking the case study children to teach their peers how to write Chinese, Arabic and Spanish using their own work. The authors found that in this bi-scriptal experience each script is a different 'mode' and the child organizes the Chinese and Arabic scripts in terms of spatiality and directionality.

A recent issue of the *International Journal of Multilingualism* focused on the concept of 'linguistic landscape'. An illustration of such research is that by Cenoz and Gorter (2006), who compare 975 signs on two streets in the Netherlands and Spain respectively on the basis of type of sign, number and names of languages on the sign, order of languages, type of font and whether the sign represents top-down language policy or bottom-up language use. Such literature perceives biliteracy as semiotic texts that are not just found in the classroom but also in the lifeworld of advertising, newspapers, comics, television, movies and other textual practices that influence school-going children.

In similar studies both Bhatia and Ritchie (2004) and Ladousa (2002) write about Hindi–English advertising in India. Bhatia and Ritchie (2004: 513) hypothesize: 'The economic forces of globalization together with the rise of global media have set the stage for a dramatic, exponential rise in global bilingualism', thus challenging Phillipson's idea of English language hegemony. Ladousa's data come from the city of Banaras where she finds that the English-only advertisements in the Roman script signal a global language of the center, whereas the Hindi ones in the Devanagari script index either a powerless periphery or an emerging Hindu/Hindi power that resists the linguistic colonization of English.

The literature on linguistic landscape does not use the term 'biliteracy', preferring 'bilingualism' as a catch-all that accommodates speech and text. However, changes in the linguistic ecology of the globalizing world and medium of instruction demand a closer look at biliteracy so as to define it in terms of specific texts and practices as well as enrich existing theory. I propose that biliterate texts can be categorized as traditionally biliterate or hybrid. A biliterate text is an artifact, for instance a road sign, piece of writing in the classroom, an advertisement on the street or graffiti, and finally an English text book that has been glossed and annotated in Hindi, in which there is written or symbolic (as in an image) evidence of two or more languages or cultures. A hybrid text is a subset of biliterate texts in that it has an aesthetic, creative nature, is usually not grammatically acceptable and is popular in sites like advertising and public culture. Specifically a hybrid text represents symbolically or through a comingling of scripts, what a bilingual does through codeswitching. While the former may be accommodated inside the bilingual classroom, the latter is proscribed.

Globalization has created hybrid textual forms which are proscribed in the bilingual classroom. However these are the texts that children encounter in their multilingual lifeworlds. The challenge is for teacher education in the field of bilingualism to include an understanding of these changing textual practices and use them as a resource in the classroom. Hornberger and Vaish (2006) show, through a comparison of bilingual classrooms in India, Singapore and South Africa, how teachers use linguistic resources that the children bring to the classroom to teach the language of power.

For instance in the classroom in India the teacher uses Hindi to explain to the student that seven times two is not thirteen, though the medium and text book of instruction for Math is English.

This Study

Now that I have introduced this research project and set up its conceptual framework, it can be described in greater detail. The ensuing four chapters are organized according to the four main continua in Hornberger's (2003) Continua of Biliteracy model: the media, content, contexts and development of biliteracy. Chapter 3, on the media of biliteracy, shows how Hindi is used as a resource in the English language classroom through patterns of codeswitching in teacher talk. In terms of Hornberger's (2003) model the media of biliteracy are about the continua between divergent and convergent scripts, successive and simultaneous bilingualism, and dissimilar and similar structures. Here I link classroom practice with the mingling of languages in the lifeworld of the students, as in advertising, road signs etc. This chapter also gives the reader illustrations of biliterate and hybrid texts, which are becoming increasingly common in a globalizing India.

Chapter 4 is about what is taught in the classroom or the content of biliteracy. The three continua in this aspect of biliteracy are between the vernacular and literary, majority and minority languages, and contextualized and decontextualized literacy practices. In this chapter I analyze English and Science text books currently used in the English-medium stream in government schools, pointing to their strengths and weaknesses. Through these texts I analyze pedagogic practice in higher classes. Chapters 3 and 4 give a complete picture of pedagogy in governments schools for girls from low-income homes. This pedagogy is deeply rooted in the cultural traditions of India. Finally I show how teachers link literacy practices in and outside the classroom.

Chapter 5 is about the contexts of biliteracy. It is based on a specific part of my data set in which I tried to get at the attitudes of students towards Hindi and English. These attitudes are not simply instrumental and status related for English and solidarity related for Hindi.

Finally, Chapter 6, which is on the development of biliteracy, analyzes how much is learned and what it is used for. This chapter reports research from a call center in Delhi, which employs and trains young 'agents'. Most of these agents come from government schools in the satellite towns around Delhi. As such this chapter links biliteracy with globalization through empirical evidence based on what the linguistic requirements of the globalizing workplace in India are and how schools like the RSKV are meeting this demand.

The following diagrammatic representation of the points on Hornberger's (2003) model will be useful for those readers who are not familiar with this heuristic:

Traditionally less powerful	Traditionally more powerful
Media of biliteracy	
Simultaneous exposure	Successive exposure
Dissimilar structures	Similar structures
Divergent scripts	Convergent scripts
Content of biliteracy	
Minority	Majority
Vernacular	Literary
Contextualized	Decontextualized
Contexts of biliteracy	
Micro	Macro
Oral	Literate
Bi(multi)lingual	Monolingual
Development of biliteracy	
Reception	Production
Oral	Written
L1	L2

Mohandas Karamchand Gandhi's (1869–1948) Relevance for Biliteracy and Globalization

Gandhi was a prolific writer and produced a massive body of newspaper articles, speeches and letters, not to mention his numerous witticisms, many of which have not been written down and are circulated amongst Indians like modern mythology. For instance, when asked by a BBC reporter what he thought of Western civilization, he is supposed have said that it would be a good idea. He wrote in Gujerati, Hindi and English, and I have read his work in Hindi and English. His opinions on religion, education, politics, celibacy, vegetarianism, modernity and industrialization are deceptively simple. What is unique about Gandhi as a social scientist is that all his ideas are infused with a spiritualism that is difficult to call Hinduism as he draws his religious ideas from disparate people like Ruskin and Tolstoy. In fact according to Young (2001: 33) Gandhi's spirituality is the reason that he is not taken seriously as a social scientist: 'Such is his sanctified status that much of the literature on Gandhi tends to be devotional rather than analytical, abstracting his thought and beliefs while downplaying the material aspects of his political practices'.

Nandy (1995) rightly notes that Gandhi thought of himself as a scientist, though with an alternative view of science and modernity. Gandhi's autobiography (Gandhiji (1957)) is called *My Experiments With Truth*, in which the use of the word 'experiment' emphasizes Gandhi's stance as a social scientist. Gandhi linked social development of the scientist's work in India by 'reaffirming the scientific role of the humble craftsman embedded in the folk traditions' (Nandy, 1995: 183). He was against vivisection and believed that a human being should conduct experiments only on his own body, which is what Gandhi's autobiography is about. In this book Gandhi explores the ecological value of vegetarianism, abstinence and a social structure that is based on the village and not the city.

Gandhi's spiritual status makes him far less cited amongst Euro-American scholars than, for instance, Paulo Freire, though their ideas were similar. Freire's (1971) work with peasant groups in Brazil and Chile showed how education can lead to the emancipation of the poor, an idea that Gandhi used amongst low caste groups or the 'untouchables'. Both Freire and Gandhi wrote about a critical social praxis. Similarly Gandhi is not considered to be in the same genre of social scientists as Bernstein and Bourdieu by the international academic community. In cases where Gandhi's educational ideas are highlighted, it is in the realm of nonformal education (Ramanathan, 2006b) and this has the value of bringing Gandhi's ideas before international sociolinguists and educationalists who are not familiar with Gandhi's work. My research moves that process forward by introducing key words from Gandhi's work like Sarvodaya and Shram into the field of language and education. These ideas are part of the mainstream national school system of India.

The only Euro-American scholar in the field of education who has acknowledged the impact of Gandhi is Spring (2001). Spring comments that Gandhi's nonviolent methods of resistance had an enormous impact on Martin Luther King Jr, thus India's independence movement had a ripple effect on ending school segregation in the USA. Through a discussion of Nehru, Ambedkar and Gandhi, Spring compares the caste system in India to the segregation of African–Americans in the USA. He shows that through the global flow of ideas, Gandhi was influenced by Tolstoy and Ruskin, the Bhagwat Gita and the Theosophical Society, all of which helped him formulate his ideas about an egalitarian society. Gandhi agreed with Tolstoy that the model of schooling that originated in Europe was the main mechanism through which the industrialized modern state exploits its population. Gandhi, on the other hand, envisioned a school system where the main goal was to inculcate spirituality, strong character, truth and emancipation through the dignity of sustained access to labor and wages.

The last chapter of this book will show how the globalizing workplace offers dignity of labor, or what Gandhi called 'shram', to the urban disadvantaged. For this social group schooling is inextricably linked to work and Gandhi himself was in favor of the vocationalization of secondary education. Gandhi also had forceful ideas about bilingual education, which have influenced the TLF of India described in Chapter 1. According to the TLF the three languages in the curriculum of the child are supposed to provide both spiritual development through the study of classical languages like Sanskrit and Arabic along with the mother tongue, and access to linguistic and economic capital through English.

Conclusion

This chapter has defined and problematized the key terms of this book: biliteracy and globalization. It has also shown the confluence of biliteracy and globalization as a relatively new subfield in sociolinguistics where there are new types of texts, literacy events and where the teaching and learning of language is instrumentalized towards specific sectors of the economy. Globalization is a highly contested site and opposing views on this inexorable process have been described within which the author takes a stance. Another key term that has been introduced is Mohandas Karamchand Gandhi's 'Sarvodaya', on which the chain of RSKVs are founded. The relationship of 'Sarvodaya' with biliteracy and globalization has been alluded to with the promise of expansion in later chapters. Finally, the organization of the book on the basis of the Continua of Biliteracy has been summarized.

Chapter 3

In What Languages is English Taught?

Hindi and English are the media of biliteracy in the RSKV. These two languages have divergent scripts, Devanagari and Roman, and dissimilar structures. Some of the structural differences between English and Hindi are that the former is SVO with a fixed word order and the latter has free word order (Mohanan, 1994); Hindi does not use articles and all nouns have gender. In terms of script there are no capital letters in Hindi and vowels can appear either as letters on their own or as marks on a consonant. In terms of spatiality, Hindi letters are written hanging off of the line on top unlike the roman script where the letters sit on the line. Thus Hindi cannot be written in those lined copy books where there are both blue and red lines for the capital and small letters respectively of the Roman script. Sometimes children in the RSKV bring the wrong copy book to class and then find it difficult to complete the writing task.

Pedagogic Practice in Primary Classes

Amarjeet is teaching a Grade 3 English class (field notes, 4 April 2004). Though it is about 37°C and sunny outside, the classroom seems dark. The 35 girls in this class sit in twos on run-down desks and chairs. The walls are cracked with peeling paint and the floor is dusty. There are no charts or pictures on the walls. On one side of the classroom is the door and a stray dog outside is rummaging in a pile of waste. There is a problem regarding stray dogs in the school and the teachers have warned me to be careful. On the other side is a barred window, which overlooks the school's high boundary wall, making the classroom look somewhat like a prison. The girls in this class are about 8 years old, but to me they look around 4 or 5 due to different nutritional practices. All the children are in their uniform – a gray skirt, white blouse, gray tie and socks and shoes. The girls with long hair wear two braids, each folded into two and tied at the head, extremely tightly, with a white ribbon. Many girls wear a bindi (a red dot in the middle of their foreheads worn by Hindu women). For a look inside the classrooms of the RSKV see Photos 1 and 2 in Appendix 3.

The lesson from the English text book is about a girl called Cheena who has been selected for the school play and is excitedly telling her mother about it.

Transcript 1

1.	**Amarjeet:**	मै read करूंगी । आप सुनना । मैं हिन्दी में भी बोलूंगी । ठीक है? समझ में आ गया? बात नहीं करोगे । बस सुनोगे ।
	Amarjeet:	*I will read. You listen. I will also speak in Hindi. OK? Understand? You will not talk. You will only listen.*
2.	**Amarjeet:**	Keep fit miss.
3.	**Class:**	Keep fit miss.
4.	**Amarjeet:**	I have
5.	**Class:**	I have
6.	**Amarjeet:**	Good news.
7.	**Class:**	Good news.
8.	**Amarjeet:**	मेरे पास एक अच्छी खबर है । चीना आई और बोली Mummy Mummy एक अच्छी खबर है । What is it?
	Amarjeet:	*I have a piece of good news. Cheena came and said, 'Mummy, Mummy, there is a piece of good news.' 'What is it?'*
9.	**Class:**	What is it?
10.	**Amarjeet:**	कया है?
	Amarjeet:	What is it?
11.	**Class:**	कया है?
	Class:	What is it?
12.	**Amarjeet:**	Asked her mother. उसकी Mummy ने पूछा । I have been.
	Amarjeet:	*Asked her mother. Her Mummy asked. I have been…*
13.	**Class:**	I have been.
14.	**Amarjeet:**	Selected.
15.	**Class:**	Selected.
16.	**Amarjeet:**	as
17.	**Class:**	as
18.	**Amarjeet:**	the Rani of
19.	**Class:**	the Rani of
20.	**Amarjeet:**	Jhansi
21.	**Class:**	Jhansi
22.	**Amarjeet:**	In my school play.
23.	**Class:**	In my school play.
24.	**Amarjeet:**	School में program होता है ना? आपको भी याद होगा….वो कहती है मेरे को select किया है…She said proudly.
	Amarjeet:	*In the school there are programs right? You will recall… She says I have been selected….She said proudly.*

At the end of this lesson Amarjeet explains to me what she does after she has taught in this way:

Transcript 2

Words मैं underline करवाती हूँ । फिर word meanings लिखवा के याद करने को कहती हूँ । अगर ये मैं हिन्दी में question बोलूँ तो बता देंगे बच्चे । पर इनहे लिखना नहीं आएगा । इस question में 'teacher' word बोल देंगे । 'Why' वाला question मुश्किल है इनके लिये ।

Words I get underlined. Then I get the word meanings written and tell them to memorize. If I ask them a question in Hindi they will be able to tell me the answer. But they won't be able to write. In (answer to) this question the 'teacher' word they can say. 'Why' questions are difficult for them.

Choral recitation

The pedagogic practice of choral recitation hits the reader in Transcript 1. For instance from Lines 13 to 23 Amarjeet makes the class recite the sentence: 'I have been selected as the Rani of Jhansi in my school play'. The recitation is broken into the smallest units and in lines 16 and 17 the class even recites the word 'as'. From the perspective of ELT in countries where English is spoken as a first language this will look like mindless chanting without comprehension. However, this is a culturally situated pedagogy that is ecologically harmonious with the contexts of biliteracy that the children bring to the classroom. In the case of the oral-literate continuum, both ends are highly respected in the Indian context. The Vedic, and indeed the Koranic, traditions valorize correct pronunciation and chanting of *shlokas* or verses. Alexander (2000), whose database includes pedagogic practice in India, rightly comments that there is a longevity of culturally situated pedagogies that can be seen in many countries even in today's classrooms. In Amarjeet's classroom we see a pedagogic practice that is rooted in a 5000-year-old tradition of memorization and 'learning'.

Wright (2001) sees a similar pedagogy in the Grade 1 and 2 classrooms of Ghinda, Eritrea, and concludes that analyzing such a practice from a Western lens is not constructive. She writes that such a pedagogic practice allows the children to practice new words and expressions, encourages discipline, fosters camaraderie and creates a nonevaluative forum where the child is not scared to speak up. The same skills are being encouraged and values being upheld in Amarjeet's classroom. The girls in her class speak practically no English outside the classroom as they live in a very Hindi/Punjabi/Urdu-speaking environment. Thus the classroom is the only 'enunciative space' they have in which to practice the English they learn. Also, this is the way Amarjeet creates class participation as asking the children a question in English will only silence the subaltern.

Simultaneous translation

Another distinctive aspect of this transcript is that of simultaneous translation that Amarjeet provides for her students. For instance in Transcript 1, Line 8, Amarjeet offers a translation of what has gone before. Line 10 is a translation of Line 9. Line 24 is part translation part explanation.

This practice is in keeping with what Mrs. Dhingra, a high school English teacher in the SKV, calls the 'indirect method'. The following comment explains what she means by this term (field notes, 28 March 2005):

Transcript 3

This is the real life situation. तुम जितना मरजी direct method करा लो. When they come to 6th class and they start ABCD इनका दिमाग तो हिन्दी में ही चलता है । I don't think without translation method there can be any success. क्योंकी मैने देखा है they don't understand until and unless I tell them something in हिन्दी। तनखा मुझे सरकार दे रही है पर जब तक मेरा पढाया मेरे बच्चों को समझ में नहीं आता तो I think मैं तो उनके लिये zero हूँ ।

This is the real life situation. You can do the direct method as much as you want. When they come to 6th class and they start ABCD their brain works only in Hindi. I don't think without translation method there can be any success. Because I have seen they don't understand until and unless I tell them something in Hindi. The government is giving me my salary but until my children understand what I have taught them, I think I am a zero for them.

In my conversation with Mrs. Dhingra she mentioned that she herself was trained in the translation method. In the same interview she remarked:

I'm in favor of translation method. Because maybe I myself have this training in translation method. And due to that only our English is OK and our Hindi is OK.

Though Mrs. Dhingra is referring to Hindi-medium children who formally start English only in Grade 6 under the Three Language Formula (TLF), this is the pedagogic practice in the English-medium stream too, as can be seen in Amarjeet's English-medium class. In Mrs. Dhingra's view this is best practice for government schools in India because the children come from non-English-speaking homes. Also the home does not have the kind of social and linguistic capital that the child needs to make a smooth transition into the biliterate classroom. Her professional view is 'Go from known to unknown. But you cannot go from unknown to known' (field notes, 28 March 2005).

My interview with the head of elementary education at the National Council for Educational Research and Training (NCERT) (field notes, 20 June 2001), Dr. K.K. Vashishtha, and his assistant Shefali, confirmed the method advocated by Mrs. Dhingra. The NCERT produces all the text books used in the national school system in India. Dr. Vashishtha said that though the text books incorporate the communicative approach, this cannot be the main focus of the text given the background of the children using these texts. These texts are created for second-, sometimes third-, language users. In these texts 'the vocabulary, materials and culture are controlled' (field notes, 20 June 2001). Dr. Vashishtha also informed me that in many primary schools Social Studies is taught in Hindi even in the English medium. This is because Social Studies will require a firm grounding in English, which many of the children do not have. They might know enough English to deal with Math and Science but not enough to study Social Studies in English. Thus he encourages the schools to decide whether they want Social Studies in English or Hindi even in the English-medium stream.

According to Jacobson (1990) language distribution across the curriculum and subjects is what determines the methodology of the bilingual program. In his research, of the 10 ways of mixing languages in a bilingual program, he conducted a longitudinal study only on two: the New Concurrent Approach (in which the two languages are used concurrently) and the Language Separation Approach (in which one subject is taught only in one language). His findings were that children in both streams did well and these were successful language distribution practices. In a similar study Hornberger (1990a), who compared a bilingual program (Spanish and Quechua) with a non-bilingual program (Spanish only) in Peru, found that the former resulted in better language acquisition in the mother tongue, Quechua, which then led to better acquisition of the school language, Spanish.

In the RSKV the language distribution practice at the policy level is that Math, Science and English are in English, and Hindi and Social Studies are in Hindi, which according to Baker (2006) would be a 60:40 dual language program. However, in the classrooms described herein the media of biliteracy jostle, contest and network with each other in multiple patterns. In fact, of Jacobson's 10 types of language mixing, in the RSKV I see 4 or 5 in the same class period. According to

Khubchandani (2003), there are three such interactions between media. The first is passive and active media where the students are lectured in one language but write in another. The second is formal and informal media where formal teaching in the class is in one language but explanations are provided in another. And finally there is the multitier media where the medium of instruction in the primary school is in the mother tongue but in secondary school the child encounters a new media of instruction. In Transcript 1 Amarjeet is using English and Hindi as formal and informal media respectively. She uses her ability to codeswitch to maximize the use of both media in the classroom. Amarjeet's approach in Transcript 1 is restricted to using multiple media in speech; however, in the following lesson I will show that this approach is also the pedagogic practice in literacy.

Porous boundaries between Hindi and English

Radha is teaching the Grade 1 English-medium class (field notes, 19 November 1999). The 38 children sit on the floor on jute mats as there are no desks and chairs in this class. Their bags and water bottles are beside them. Radha is correcting English copy books and her instructions to the class are that while she is completing the corrections they should read their Hindi books. Most of the children are reading diligently in pairs or groups of three. I cannot see anyone reading alone. Some are copying what Radha has written on the board. A few children are distracted and spend their time spooning dust into a paper cone that they have made. The blackboard has been divided into two parts. On the left Radha has written some scrambled words in English and the corresponding correct words:

Lesson 25

Make words

sggs	eggs
anmgo	mango
leapp	apple
soptman	postman
ysbo	boys

On the right-hand side of the blackboard the teacher has written some words in Hindi with the appropriate drawing:

Drawing
आँख (*eyes*)
चाँद (*moon*)

धनुष   (*bow*) [as in bow and arrow]
छाता   (*umbrella*)
झाड़ू   (*broom*)

When I asked Radha whether this was the English or the Hindi period, she seemed confused. She pointed out that she does not divide the periods in the day in this way; her day is divided according to task. As in the present lesson she often makes them do Hindi and English tasks together. She also points out that as these children are small they often do not bring the correct copy book to school. This is very important because the Hindi and English copy books have different lines. As I have explained in the beginning of this chapter, this is so because of the different ways in which the Devanagari and Roman scripts are written. Radha finds that if she is very strict about allocating time to discrete languages, many of the children will not be able to complete the task because they have brought the wrong copy book to class. Thus she finds it far more productive not to make these artificial boundaries between languages.

Thus there is a seamless fluidity in media of biliteracy in the RSKV. The teachers do not make a clear distinction between the English and Hindi periods; instead, one networks with the other without artificial boundaries. Especially in the primary classes the children are allowed to access multiple points on the continua of the media of biliteracy. This is a somewhat unique method of allocating time to a particular language in the classroom. Ramanathan (2005) shows that the English text books in the state of Gujerat actually support this seamlessness between languages and encourage the teacher to use the home language in the English classroom by giving her explicit instructions to do so.

In keeping the isoglosses between languages porous the teachers find that the mother tongue is a great resource in the English language classroom. The following transcript illustrates this pedagogic practice:

Transcript 4

Like Amarjeet, Aruna is also an experienced primary school teacher. She is teaching her Grade 5 English-medium class a lesson on Holi, a Hindu festival of North India in which people celebrate the onset of spring by throwing color on each other (field notes 6 April 2004).

1. **Aruna:**   ...सीधे बैठ जाओ
   Aruna: ...*Sit properly*
2. **Student:** (Reads from the text.) They were playing color on the terrace on Holi...They look down and see a man walking on the street. Ramesh ...color on him.

3.	**Aruna:**	Terrace माने?
	Aruna:	*Terrace means?*
4.	**Class:**	छत
5.	**Aruna:**	वो कया कर रहे थे
	Aruna:	*What were they doing?*
6.	**Class:**	होली खेल रहे थे
	Class:	*They were playing Holi*
7.	**Aruna:**	और उन्होने क्या देखा?
	Aruna:	*And what did they see?*
8.	**Class:**	आदमी सड़.क पर चल रहा था
	Class:	*A man was walking on the street.*
9.	**Student:**	Ma'am 'pour'.
10.	**Aruna:**	पानी उडे.लना
	Aruna:	*pour*
11.	**Student:**	Ramesh and Geeta poured the color on him and…in the street…
12.	**Aruna:**	Street means?
13.	**Class:**	गली
14.	**Aruna:**	नहीं street माने सड़क। And they lophed. Loph माने?
15.	**Class:**	Hasna.
16.	**Aruna:**	क्या करते हैं वो लोग अजनबी आदमी के साथ
	Aruna:	*What do they do with the stranger?*
17.	**Student:**	(reads) 'That is very bad. You must not throw colors on strangers.'
18.	**Aruna:**	Strangers means?
19.	**Class:**	अजनबी
20.	**Aruna:**	That is not good. आपको किसी भी अजनबी के साथ ऐसे नहीं करना चाहिए
	Aruna:	*That is not good. You should not behave in this way with strangers*
21.	**Student:**	(reads) '…should go and say sorry to that man.'
22.	**Aruna:**	वो अपनी Mummy से कया पूछते हैं? की?
	Aruna:	*What do they ask their Mummy? That?*
22.	**Class:**	हम उनसे sorry कह के आएं
	Class:	*We should go and say sorry*
23.	**Student:**	(reads) '..We should not throw color on strangers.
24.	**Aruna:**	तो वो कहते हैं कि जाओ उनसे माफी मांगो। और वो आदमी कहता है कि आपको ऐसे color नहीं फेंकना चाहिए। अपने घर मे ही खेलना चाहिए।
	Aruna:	*So they say that go and say sorry. And the man says that you should not throw color like this. You should play in your own house*

Using mother tongue as a resource

In this transcript Aruna begins by making a child stand up and read a large chunk of text aloud. What follows after the reading is mainly in Hindi. Aruna checks if the children are familiar with the vocabulary like 'terrace', 'street', 'laugh' and 'strangers'. In some cases the children ask for word meanings, for example, in Line 9 a student asks for the meaning of 'pour', which Aruna supplies in Hindi. The pattern of interaction is the well known Initiation Response Evaluation (IRE), only in this case there is no evaluation. When Aruna gets the desired response she moves on without any evaluative comment or phrase. This aspect of interacting with children is a culturally contextualized socialization practice, as Indian children are not praised excessively by their parents and elders. In Lines 5 and 7 she asks questions in Hindi to make sure that the children are following the action of the story. As this is a large class of about 40 girls Aruna prefers a whole class response and does not nominate anyone for an answer except for reading.

In this IRE pattern there is a codeswitch from I to R, especially when Aruna is teaching vocabulary. For instance in Line 18 Aruna asks a question in English and the class replies in Hindi in Line 19. This pattern is also discernable in Lines 12 and 13. When Aruna is checking comprehension both the initiation from her and the response from the class is in Hindi. For instance in Line 22 she asks the class: 'what do the children ask their mother? That?'. In Line 23 the class responds in Hindi while borrowing the English word 'sorry'.

Finally there is a strong push towards memorization of lexical items, which is emphasized in Transcript 2 and illustrated in Transcript 4. In Transcript 2 Amarjeet emphasizes that once she has taught the lesson in this way she makes the students underline the key words, translate them and then memorize the meanings. Thus she is trying to build the basic vocabulary of these children as they might not have access to English books at home which they read for pleasure. Transcript 4 shows that Aruna has the same view and building vocabulary is one of the foundations of her pedagogy. Like choral recitation memorization is also a culturally situated pedagogy in a country where in the religious domain it is common for adults and children to memorize large chunks of texts without knowing the meanings of every single word.

This is what Kumaravadivelu (1994) calls the pedagogy of post-methodism in which teachers in periphery communities develop their own pedagogical paradigms. The classrooms in the RSKV are not the site where, for instance, extended oral narratives in the target language can successfully be practiced. In fact using such pedagogies in Amarjeet's class will disenfranchise and alienate the children as 'From the point of view of these student groups and communities, process methods are based on the linguistic needs of the dominant community (in L1 contexts) whose students have the required codes/skills and simply need to develop higher level skills of usage though active interaction and participation' (Canagarajah, 2002: 139). Similarly Delpit (2001) rightly points out that children in disadvantaged groups lack the physical resources, like the requisite texts and audio-visual aids, and the very codes required to participate in such Centre-based pedagogies. Thus they first need a firm grounding in basic skills, which may in fact be through a translation method.

Codeswitching

On a sunny April morning (field notes, 5 April 2005), I am sitting with a group of seven teachers, most of them from the primary school, on the verandah of the school. They have welcomed me with a glass of strong, sticky, sweet tea. They are talking about timetables for their classes.

Transcript 5

1.	Amarjeet:	Time table set कर लिया?
	Amarjeet:	*Have you set the time table?*
2.	Priya:	अच्छा क्या था? I didn't see it.
	Priya:	*Ok what was it? I didn't see it.*
3.	Amarjeet:	दो periods जो हैं वो drawing और art and craft के होने चाहिएं । Games नहीं हो पाता गरमी की वजह से ।
	Amarjeet:	*2 periods should be for drawing and art and craft. We cannot have games because of the heat.*

This conversation amongst the teachers shows a high level of code-mixing, -switching and borrowing considered unmarked by bilinguals in Delhi. The literature on codeswitching is too vast to review here. I take as a definition of these terms Ritchie and Bhatia's (2004) suggestion that codeswitching is intersentential and codemixing intrasentential. As they do not mention borrowing as separate category, I would like to add Kamwangamalu's (1992) definition that, structurally unlike codemixing and codeswitching, borrowing entails integration of linguistic units from one language into the linguistic system of the other language. Borrowing may occur in the speech of either monolinguals or bilinguals, whereas codemixing and codeswitching can only be done by bilinguals.

Lines 1 and 2 of Transcript 5 are illustrations of codemixing and codeswitching respectively. Amarjeet asks her colleague, 'Time table set

कर लिया?', in an utterance where the part of the verb phrase is in Hindi. In reply Priya uses two sentences but switches codes between the two: 'अच्छा क्या था? I didn't see it.' In Line 3 of this transcript Amarjeet borrows the English lexical items 'periods', 'drawing', 'art and craft' and 'games' into Hindi sentences. The point of this discussion on codeswitching is that such utterances are the way bilinguals in Delhi speak in their normal conversations, thus codeswitching in the classroom is not marked. The following comment by Mr. Kalra, the high school Math teacher, who teaches Math in both Hindi and English, is an illustration of language attitudes in Delhi. He says about Hindi and English:

> हिन्दी हमारी mother tongue है । पर आज की date में आप उनको दोनो को mother tongue कहोगे । (field notes, 28 March 2005)

> *Hindi is our mother tongue. But in today's day and age both will be called mother tongues.*

According to Lin (2001), using multiples codes in an English-medium class is a form of linguistic and academic brokerage. Analyzing transcripts from secondary school classrooms in Hong Kong, Lin discusses the motivations of teachers for switching from English to Cantonese and vice versa. She finds that Cantonese is used to annotate the English lesson and thus bridge the home school chasm. Similarly, in my transcripts Amarjeet, Aruna and Mrs. Dhingra use Hindi to translate, annotate and explain the English lesson. They are thus brokering the English-medium education for students who would otherwise have a problem accessing the language and the content of the lesson.

Biliterate and Hybrid Texts in the Lifeworld of Delhi

Just as multiple codes are used simultaneously in bilingualism, so are they used in biliteracy creating biliterate and hybrid texts. These terms have been defined in Chapter 2. Here I will give illustrations of such texts and analyze them. Figure 3.1 is an illustration of a biliterate text and as such this artifact is comparable to the photo of the road sign on the cover of this book.

In biliterate signs like this all translations are provided for the viewer and they are self-explanatory. The languages in such texts are deliberately kept discrete and mingling is proscribed, giving them a somewhat top-down quality. Such signs are common in government and school documents and have a formal, artificial feel about them, while at the same time it is clear to the reader that such a text is officially sanctioned by an institution with power like the state or the school. Another illustration of

Figure 3.1 Sign above the laboratory in the RSKV

such a text would be the Hindi/English exit card that an arriving passenger has to fill out before leaving the Indira Gandhi International Airport in New Delhi.

On the other hand, Figures 3.2 and 3.3 are hybrid texts. The mark of a hybrid text, like the one in Figure 3.2, is the intermeshing of scripts and languages such that prizing them apart causes loss of meaning. The main heading on this photo is संडे नवभारत टाइम्स, meaning 'Sunday Navbharat Times', written in Devanagari, though the words 'Sunday' and 'Times' are English words. The Hindi word for Sunday is 'Itvaar', but the newspaper chooses not to use this. Immediately under the main heading is a block of text, divided into three, where both Devanagari and Roman scripts are used. Whereas 'Hello Delhi' and 'NBT Property' is in Roman, the text under this is in Devanagari. Finally the main news item in this paper (in bold Devanagari above the smiley face) is लाइफ स्टाइल से तय होगा कार का प्रीमियम, which can be transliterated as 'Life style se teya hogaa car kaa premium'. In this headline the words 'life', 'style', 'car' and 'premium' are English words written in Devanagari characters.

There are two types of codemixing going on in the text in Figure 3.2. At one level there is the use of English words. The reasons for codemixing in this hybrid text are complex. In the case of 'life style' and 'premium', the audience is unlikely to know the Hindi equivalent of these words, thus the writer has used the English word itself. However this is not the

Figure 3.2 From *The Navbharat Times*

Figure 3.3 Advertisement for tea

case for words like 'car' and 'Sunday', where the equivalent Hindi words 'gaadi' and 'itvaar' are widely used. Here there is codemixing in the script itself (English words being written in Devanagari), leading to the creation of a hybrid text. The reason for this hybridity is the audience of this newspaper, which is Hindi dominant but English knowing. News stories on aspects of a modern urban lifestyle like car ownership, fitness, etc. tend to be hybrid in their style and thus give the newspaper a trendy image.

The children in the RSKV are used to seeing such biliterate and hybrid texts in their lifeworlds. In most homes in Delhi biliterate artifacts are strewn all over the house, from a phone bill which is in English on one side and Hindi on the other, to a carton of juice on which both Roman and Devanagari scripts are intermeshed. In the last quarter of 2005 one of the Bollywood songs to hit the top in the Indian charts was 'इश्क दी गली विच no entry', meaning 'In the lane of love there is "no entry"'(www.raga. com). This song is in the liminal spaces between Hindi, Urdu, Punjabi and English, and the words are so intermeshed that it is impossible to detect where one language stops and another begins. Kachru (2006) analyzes Hindi–English mixing in Bollywood movies to show that this is an act of playfulness with which the song satirizes, exoticizes and jokes about lifestyles of English-speaking Indians. According to the dimensions of the media of biliteracy, though the children of the RSKV are successively exposed to English, because they encounter it formally only when they come to school, they are simultaneously exposed to English in their lifeworld.

This mixing of English and Hindi in the linguistic landscape of North India is the mark of a globalizing country. Bhatia & Ritchie (2004), in an essay on bilingualism in advertising, though they don't make a fine distinction between biliterate and hybrid texts as I am doing here, write that it is in the interest of companies to capture a larger share of the market by creating biliterate advertisements. The authors also use these advertisements to make an important point about the use of non-English languages, a point that is crucial for this book. They comment that: 'Although the global dominance of English is self-evident, and is growing rapidly, it is premature to claim that other major languages of the world are dying and English is the killer language. In fact, the ten most widely spoken languages of the world are rapidly catching up with English in the arena of global electronic communication and media' (Bhatia & Ritchie, 2004: 519).

Thus, as I have outlined in the previous chapter on the conceptual framework of this book, globalization is not only the story of the spread of global English, although this is the story that we hear the most. Globalization is also the story of the rise of non-English languages, through domains like advertising, and, indeed, even the Internet. In India if multinationals advertise only in English they will not only capture a very small English-speaking population but also appear colonial and stultified. Bhatia and Ritchie point to an inherent creativity in bilinguals which motivates them to use multiple codes and not a lack of fluency in either language, making hybrid advertisements and other such tests look youthful, trendy and current.

The advertisement in Figure 3.3 is another illustration of a hybrid text. This advertisement for the extremely popular Red Label tea in India seems to be mainly in English. However the last line in the top half reads 'Ab Pyaar ka Pyala, Sehat Wala', which is a transliteration of the Hindi for, 'Now a cup of love, with health'. On the second half of the page the font looks like Devanagari but this is a creative way of displaying the Roman script to look like Devanagari. The lines read, 'nature's secrets for your family's health'. The line drawn across the top of the letters gives the impression that this line is in Devanagari. Furthermore some letters are also hybridized to create a fusion of both the Roman and Devanagari scripts. For instance the letter 's' in the words 'nature's', 'secrets' and 'family's' is written to resemble the short vowel 'इ' in Hindi.

Advertising is thus a site for the creation of all types of hybridity in script, font and language. This is very much a bottom-up phenomenon where texts are created that are considered trendy and cool rather than official and authoritative. In speech the same style is used by TV hosts who mix Hindi, English, Punjabi and even Sanskrit with lightening speed, engaging millions of multilingual speakers by their verbal pyrotechnics.

Conclusions

This chapter has described and analyzed pedagogic practice in primary classes of the RSKV. These practices valorize choral recitation, memorization, the IRE participant structure though without much evaluation and the use of mother tongue as a resource in the English classroom. Interviews with the teachers show that this pedagogic practice is chosen by the teachers in keeping with the cultural context of the RSKV and the resources that the children bring to the classroom. In not keeping English and Hindi discrete in the enacted curriculum the teachers are creating a bridge between the lifeworld of the bilingual student and the English-language classroom. In this lifeworld Hindi and English mingle to produce hybrid texts that are a mark of a globalizing economy. Rather than the spread of global English this chapter emphasizes that globalization is also about the rise of non-English languages as they are used by multinationals to increase their market share.

The dimensions of the media of biliteracy valorize all varieties but along with access to standard forms of the same. This bidialectalism in the school is very important in cases where the students are being educated in, for instance, standard Castilian Spanish, whereas they might speak a Puerto Rican variety at home. The teacher who valorizes both varieties of Spanish provides more agency and voice to all the learners in her classroom. Delpit (2001) gives some excellent examples of how teachers can teach standard English in the classroom while valorizing non-standard forms. Amarjeet achieves this by valorizing Hindi, the home language of most of the children. Through systematic codeswitching she paves the way for content transfer from English to Hindi. She uses the standard form of both languages, thus making sure that the input that the children get in school is of high quality. This is very important for the urban disadvantaged because even the Hindi they might hear in their neighborhoods might not be standard.

Chapter 4
What is Taught?

The arguments of this chapter are framed around the 'content of biliteracy'. Within the parameters of the content of biliteracy the minority, vernacular and contextualized ends of the continua have been traditionally less powerful. For instance dialects of Hindi like Bhojpuri and Magadhi are minority languages that are not included in the school system in India. Though Bhojpuri and Magadhi have a great literary tradition, they are subsumed under Hindi in the Indian census. On the other hand, Hindi and English are majority languages. In Hornberger's (2003) model the word 'majority' does not necessarily mean number of speakers as the number of speakers for English in India will be low. The word carries connotations of power and how this is distributed in the form of access to linguistic capital. In this sense both Hindi and English, are 'majority' languages with great literary traditions that can carry the decontextualized meanings of the curriculum.

This chapter analyzes text books being used in the English-medium stream in government schools in India. As it is not possible to cover all the text books, I have focused on Science and English texts. Through an analysis of the texts I show pedagogic practice in the higher classes and highlight the differences with primary school pedagogy. There is focus on how an experienced teacher deals with an archaic lesson in the classroom. I extend the discussion from the previous chapters to show the kinds of biliterate and hybrid texts that children produce in and out of the classroom and discuss the implications of these literacy practices.

The page in Figure 4.1 is from NCERT (1989), a science text book for Grade 5. From a chapter titled 'Communicable Diseases', these pictures and the text under it sensitize children about ways in which they can catch diseases from their environment. The first paragraph on the right page reads:

> Garbage thrown here and there also decays. Flies breed in such decaying matter. They also sit on exposed excreta or stool. Then they carry the germs. When they sit on the exposed food it gets contaminated. Thus these germs infect the food. (p. 59)

Figure 4.1 A page from a science text book

The pictures on this page are in keeping with the environment of the urban disadvantaged and the rural poor. In the picture on the right the reader can see activities related to water: a man is washing clothes, a boy is bathing and another man is washing a buffalo. There are two women on the right: one is bringing water home from a community tap and the other is cleaning utensils. The poor do not necessarily have access to running water in their homes. Many of them have to get water from a community tap and store it at home in buckets. In many families children are given the task of queuing up at the community tap to collect water in buckets, a task that can take hours depending on the length of the queue.

Critical Thinking

The lesson attempts to create awareness about the relationship between disease and sanitation in first-generation learners whose parents might not have had formal schooling. Also, the simplified syntax of the sentences indicates that the text book is written for a second language learner. Despite the short sentences and controlled vocabulary, the text tries to inculcate the scientific spirit of inquiry and challenges dogma. At the beginning of the same lesson the text reads:

Some believed diseases to be caused by evil spirits, omens, curses, etc. In order to prevent diseases and check epidemics people often worship, offer gifts, in kind or cash and even sacrifice living things to satisfy the evil spirits.

Scientists worked for many years to find out the causes of diseases. It was found out that diseases are actually caused by these germs. They are not caused by evil spirits as believed by some people earlier and by some even today. (NCERT, 1989: 57)

Indian newspapers often carry gory stories of fatalities due to belief in such superstitions, which are particularly common amongst the rural poor who do not have access to schooling. The text books try to strike a delicate balance by both valorizing the culture of the communities in which these books are being used, while the goal is to strike at the root of social malaise in Indian society. This type of text is particularly suitable for the learners in the RSKV as many of the children come from rural communities outside Delhi where belief in sprits and omens are part of the lifeworld of the child. I see this as a text leading to critical thinking; it is a confluence of school and community knowledges that encourages students to reinterpret their beliefs. By juxtaposing the idea that diseases are caused by evil spirits along with the alternative view that disease is caused by germs the text invites the student to re-examine belief systems.

Hornberger (2003: 52) points out that using the language of power means being able to use language in context reduced circumstances:

Within the scientific tradition and much academic writing decontextualized meanings are the meanings that count.…Being able to state truths that hold, regardless of context, has been a part of speaking the language of power (p. 52).

In the environmental science text described above, NCERT (1989), there is an extremely decontextualized chapter on eclipses. In terse scientific language the chapter conveys the main concepts in understanding eclipses and prescribes some simple activities that the children can do at home, without the use of expensive objects, to understand this phenomenon. In this chapter there is no doubt that the students are being taught English as a library language in which they can read decontextualized scientific texts. At the end of this chapter there is a list of 'Things to do' with the following point:

Ask your parents to tell you the stories related to eclipse, i.e., Rahu and Ketu. Analyze the content. Find out how scientific they are. (NCERT, 1989: 108)

Thus the text book juxtaposes community knowledge and new scientific learning and invites the child to think about it without giving any concrete answers.

Quality of Text Books

Inculcating critical thinking in India is a controversial issue and some text books do a better job than others. Ramanathan (2005) shows a lesson on eclipses from an Indian text book being used in the state of Gujerat and comments that the implicit message of this text is that traditional beliefs surrounding the phenomenon that Rahu and Ketu swallow the sun are 'strange'. In contrast, the Western scientific explanation of eclipses is normal. She comments that 'The correlation between "English", "scientific" and "correct", on the one hand, and "non-English" and "strange", on the other, and the generally "de-voicing" message this combination of phrases sends out to non-English/VM [Vernacular Medium, my brackets] students and teachers cannot be missed' (Ramanathan, 2005: 41).

Rampal (in Govinda, 2002), in a review of text books being used in India, writes that though improvements have been made, there are serious problems with Indian text books. She finds that there is a dearth of inspiring biographies of ordinary men and women. There is also no mention of cottage industries that communities have refined over the ages like the use of vegetable dyes, terracotta and block printing. She suggests that scientific and technological literacy must be linked to community practices. 'For instance, we can speak of eclipse, but must link the description to what is observed by them, and also to their existing legends about such cosmological phenomena' (in Govinda, 2002: 104). At the same time Rampal also acknowledges that there are lessons to be learned, for instance, by the text books produced by the Non Governmental Organization called Eklavya that include the beliefs of low-caste communities in the curriculum.

A similar critique of Indian text books used in government schools is made by the PROBE (1999) report. This report is the result of a massive project undertaken collaboratively by various NGOs on the status of primary schooling in India. The project team surveyed a total of 188 villages in North India using a mixed methodology. This project did not focus on English text books as English is not offered as a subject at the primary stage in rural India. The reader might recall that Ram Nivas, whose case study is presented in a previous chapter, moved from Paabi village to

Delhi for this very reason. The Probe Team found that the language of Hindi text books was dense, scientistic, alienating and many of the texts had an urban, middle-class and upper-caste bias.

These critiques of Indian text books have motivated the NCERT to undertake some major text book reforms. These reforms were also supported by the Yashpal Committee Report that brought into the headlines the 'burden of non-comprehension' that the child has to suffer due to poor quality text books (Government of India, 1993). Rampal (2007) shows how the latest Math text books produced by NCERT, called Math Magic, use photos of events that concern the life of a disadvantaged child. For instance in this conference presentation Rampal showed a page from the new text book regarding the 'kabaadiwala' or the person who comes from door to door buying used bottles, newspapers etc. The Math exercise was created around the buying and selling of such used items, which is an event close to the life world of disadvantaged children.

The recent improvements that NCERT has made have been well received by the teachers. For instance Aruna, a primary school teacher in the RSKV, thinks that the Grade 4 English text book has improved. She says:

Transcript 1

हाँ पहले तो बहुत text text था । Pictures नहीं थीं । अब Indian उसको लेकर stories हैं । पहले तो इनको बिलकुल समझ में नहीं आती थीं । मुश्किल तो इनहे अब भी होती है.. और यह सब जैसे hat में opposites दये हैं interesting बनाने के लिये ।

Yes. At first there was too much text. There were no pictures. Now there are Indian stories. First they just could not understand. Even now they face difficulties ... And like all this in a hat they have given opposites to make it more interesting. (6 April 2004)

Goals of the English Syllabus

The English text books for government high schools come in a set of three: the main text, called *English with a Purpose* (NCERT, 2002), is complimented by *Impressions*, which is a supplementary reader (NCERT, 2003a) and finally a grammar workbook called *Working With English* (NCERT, 2003b). According to NCERT the purpose of teaching English to children in government schools is the following somewhat mixed bag of skills:

- to develop need-based oral communication
- to develop ease and confidence in reading English
- to understand the overall meaning and organization of a text
- to identify the main point and supporting details
- to make inferences and assess the bias of a writer

- to argue a case
- to relate communication skills to the workplace
- to enjoy poetry. (NCERT, 2002)

Some of the goals in this set seem to contradict each other: for instance 'to develop need-based oral communication' is in opposition to 'to argue a case'. Though the former requires basic English, the latter will require a high level of fluency on the part of the speaker. In terms of the needs of students, the main goal for them is 'to relate communication skills to the workplace'. The urban disadvantaged want necessary and sufficient English competencies so that they can be trained on the job; at the same time they also want to be able to talk in English. These desires and the attitudes related to them will become clearer in the next chapter where I present the results of an open-ended survey on student attitudes.

Tickoo (1996) comments that the purpose of English in India is that it is a 'library language' and a language in which to gain scientific knowledge. For this reason teaching English communicatively is inappropriate in the Indian context. Tickoo also finds that methods and models of ELT are dominated by the monolingual world where monolingual English speakers teach those whose languages they do not know. As the primary aim in these monolingual countries is to give immigrants adequate communicative skills to survive socially in their new environment, ELT is dominated by communicative methods. Thus Tickoo (1996: 236) concludes that schools in many non-English-speaking countries need to provide for 'teaching English as the most important language of knowledge and in doing so, focus mainly on the skills and abilities that are needed to use the language in context reduced cognitive domains'.

This was, no doubt, true of English language teaching in pre-globalizing India. Today, when young people want to learn English so that they can work in a call center, it is no longer adequate to teach English only as a library language. In keeping with these demands and in an attempt to provide a need-based text book, government school texts do attempt to teach communicative skills. NCERT 2002 has a list of 10 eclectic lessons interspersed with the following 5 'conversation techniques':

- requesting and attracting attention,
- dealing with moods and feelings,
- complaining and apologizing,
- preventing interruptions and interrupting politely and
- describing people and places.

At the end of each conversational technique the class is advised to work in pairs and first rehearse the conversation provided and then change the situation and enact the scenario. They are then given a list of expressions to practice in their speech. For instance in 'requesting and attracting attention' the children are encouraged to use expressions like 'Excuse me', 'Pardon', 'I'm sorry but' and 'I would like to, but'.

Despite these communicative exercises, the children of the RSKV do not have communicative competence in English when they graduate after 12 years of English-medium education. An interview with Mrs Charu Kumar, English teacher for Classes 11 and 12, (field notes, 18 October 2005), revealed her concerns as a teacher. Her current class of 11th B is of commerce students which, she says, is a good class. Mrs Charu Kumar is not happy with the text books as these, unlike the new text books for the primary classes, have not yet been replaced with the new 'Marigold' texts that NCERT has produced. 'The language is ponderous' she says. The content of the lessons, like 'Machines and Emotions', an essay by Bertrand Russell, does not interest the children (NCERT, 2003d). They buy guides where all the questions are answered and memorize and regurgitate these in the exam.

Mrs. Charu is very concerned about such language teaching. She says that checking written work is not a pleasure because all the students have the same answer, which they have memorized from a guide. She is worried that the children are not able to express themselves. She does not think that the school has equipped them with enough English for the workplace. However, many of them take an English-speaking course after school and improve. Many of her students tell her, 'Ma'am हम आप की तरह बोलना चाहते हैं ' (Ma'am we want to talk like you). She feels bad that she is not able to give them this level of proficiency.

Grammar is a nonexaminable subject and NCERT (2003b), which is the grammar workbook, encourages the children to work with peers. The main objectives of this grammar book are to:

- practice English phonology,
- familiarize learners with the functional use of grammar and
- hone learners' reading and writing skills.

This is the weakest part of the English curriculum in government schools. The grammar workbook comes with an audio tape but I was unable to buy it at any book store. Most of the children also find that this audio tape is not available. The classrooms are not equipped with a tape player that the teacher can use. The link of this text to the other two texts in the curriculum is tenuous. Mrs Renu Chopra, who teaches English to Class XII, is also extremely disappointed with the grammar text book. She says that she finds the grammar book 'very vague' and suggests that NCERT should introduce an activity like letter writing which the students will find extremely interesting (field notes, 15 October 2005). On the other hand the supplementary reader, NCERT (2003a), is a valuable addition to this set of texts as it provides extra readings for children who live in a print-poor environment. The short stories and essays in this supplementary reader include not only non-Indian writers like Chekov and Pearl S. Buck but also Gandhi and Satyajit Ray.

Thus there have been some improvements in the text books like engaging primary school children with larger font size, less dense text and colorful pictures. In the science text books for middle school there is an inclusion of community knowledges to encourage critical thinking. However a lot more needs to be done. The high school English text books still use ponderous language and lessons that do not interest teenage children.

Pedagogic Practice in Higher Classes

Though Mrs Renu Chopra finds that many of the texts for Class 12 are good, she feels that she needs to supplement them with a discussion of real-life texts. For instance in order to teach report writing, which is a topic that usually comes in the Class 12 final exams, she uses a newspaper article from *The Times of India* about how the Central Board of Secondary Education (CBSE) will 'go soft' on marking for spelling mistakes in the upcoming exam. She gives the class instructions on how to write this report while assuming the persona of a reporter:

Transcript 2

यह हमारा introduction part हुआ । Ok? The report will be done in three parts. That is the introductory part. Introduction. Introduction is nothing but the title. ..., इसके बाद जो आपका आएगा... Next part would be content. So you write the name of the reporter over here. उसके बाद 'New Delhi'. ठीक है ? यहाँ लिखने के बाद line लगा देनी है । यह जो है, this part carries ... यह आपका one mark का होता है । उसके बाद जो आपका main part है ... this is the content ... और इसके marks होते हैं, content के, four marks होते हैं । ठीक है? Expression carries five marks. Total ten marks. .... अब जो आपका content है इसमें ... what is the discussion that we had? जो verbal inputs आपको दिए गए थे...

This is our introduction part. OK? The report will be done in three parts. That is the introductory part. Introduction. Introduction is nothing but the title ... After this what you have ... Next part would be content. So you write the name of the

reporter over here. After that 'New Delhi'. OK? Here after writing you must draw
a line. This is that ... this part carries ... This is for one mark. After this, which is
your main part ... this is the content. And the marks for this are, for content, there
are 4 marks. OK? Expression carries 4 marks. Total 10 marks ... Now inside your
content ... what is the discussion we had? The verbal inputs that had been given to
you ... (15 October 2005).

Mrs Renu Chopra's style is quite different from that of Amarjeet. Mrs
Chopra does not feel the need to directly translate every sentence as these
children are in Class 12 and have had many more years of English training. However she uses a conversational codeswitching style that does not
alienate the class. She makes sure that she subtasks the report into man-
ageable parts. For instance she says that the introduction is just the name,
title etc. and carries only one mark. The instructions are very detailed and
the class is even told that they must draw a line after the introduction. She
wants the class to concentrate more on content for which she has provided
'verbal inputs' in a previous class. By using *The Times of India* in class she
is encouraging the class to become lifelong readers of this leading English
newspaper. On the way to class she mentioned to me that though buying
this newspaper is quite expensive for these girls, she still wants to encourage them to become lifelong readers of it as this will help them improve
their English even after school.

Mrs Renu Chopra's style is a product-oriented rather than process
approach to writing. Delpit (2001) emphasizes why children of color
must be given clear instructions and the skills needed to acquire the
language of power. This is exactly what Mrs Renu Chopra is doing with
her class. She reminds the class of the 'verbal inputs' she has given them
previously and implies that those ideas must go into the content section
of the essay.

If we compare Amarjeet's style of teaching English in the primary 3
class presented in Chapter 3, Transcript 1, and Renu Chopra's style in
Class 12 presented above, it is clear that there is far less direct translation
in the latter's pedagogy. In the instructions by Renu to her class shown
above there is only one phrase that is directly translated in the whole transcript. This occurs in Line 3:

इसके बाद जो आपका आएगा ... *Next part would be ...*

Thus the scaffolding of translation is removed in the higher classes as the
English listening and speaking skills of the children improve. However,
Hindi is never completely removed from the English classes in the RSKV.
In this way the 'minority' and 'vernacular' ends of the continua are

valorized; although in the context of Delhi both Hindi and English are actually majority literary languages.

Dealing with challenging lessons in the text

Mrs Dhingra is teaching a lesson called 'On Conduct in Company' from the supplementary reader (NCERT, 2003a) to Grade 12. The lesson is a letter written by Philip Dormer Stanhope (1694–1773) who, the introduction to the lesson says, was a 'famous orator and writer', and in 1726 succeeded his father as Lord Chesterfield. The lesson is a letter that Lord Chesterfield wrote to his son advising him on how he should behave in society. In the transcript below, which is from a video, Mrs. Dhingra is focusing on the questions and answers at the end of the lesson.

Transcript 3

Mrs Dhingra:

1. अब आप question answers करो. 'Why should one not talk for long while
2. conversing with others?' One should not talk for long time when sitting in the
3. company because other person may get bored. Other person may not be interested
4. in what we are saying. So whatever you want to say you should say in short without
5. lengthy details. Other person may get very bored soon if you go on talking for a
6. long time. We should be brief and to the point. Second, 'What is Chesterfield's
7. opinion about telling stories in company?' So he says don't tell stories while sitting
8. in a company.... Avoid all the unnecessary details and come to the point and tell
9. the story in very short. But he is not in favor of telling long stories to other people.
10. 'What is the main weakness of 'long talkers' and how should it be dealt with?'
11. The main weakness of long talkers is that it shows that they cannot imagine. It
12. shows lack of imagination in those people who are talking for a long time. And

13. what they do? They … go on telling the thing. They don't know that the other
14. person may be feeling boring and what is the best way? And just give them
15. pretentious interest. Give them seeming interest. That you are interested in them
16. but don't listen to them properly. Of course it will hurt him very badly if you say
17. 'बहुत हो गया, just stop talking'. You cannot say like that. And he will be very
18. pleased if you go on listening very intently. So to deal with that you should not
19. interrupt…just pay seeming attention.…दिखाओ उसे पर सुनो नहीं क्योंकि एक
20. दम उसको बीच मे रोकना उसको बुरा feel होगा… तो उसको लगेगा कि blindly
21. कोई मेरी बात सुन रहा है । तो the main weakness of the long talker is that they
22. lack imagination…because conversation is a two way traffic we should give the
23. other person a chance to speak also … (20 December 2005)

In Transcript 3 Mrs Dhingra is taking the class through the questions at the end of the lesson. She starts in Line 1 by saying 'Now you do the question answers' and reads the first question from the text book: 'Why should one not talk for long while conversing with others?' From Lines 2 to 6 she proceeds to answer the question for the class. In Line 6 she reads the second question from the text: 'What is Chesterfield's opinion about telling stories in company?' Again she proceeds to answer this question and this goes on till Line 21 and beyond.

The main aspects of this pedagogic practice are minimal use of Hindi, the whole class lecture mode, the nature of English in teacher talk and focus on preparing for exams. Similar to the pedagogic practice of Mrs Renu Chopra in Transcript 2, here Mrs Dhingra avoids the use of Hindi as much as possible. Except in Lines 19, 20 and 21, where her utterances sound more like normal conversation, she maintains an English-only stance. In this way she provides the requisite input for her students to take notes and prepare to answer the questions in their copy books. In written work Mrs Dhingra does not allow any Hindi, thus she makes sure that she models each answer for her students the way it should appear in their copy books. At the same time Mrs Dhingra is not resorting to dictating the answers, which primary school English teachers like Amarjeet often have to do.

In this product-oriented modeling approach Mrs Dhingra begins each answer the way it should appear in an exam script. For instance in Line 2 she begins the answer to the first question using the syntax in the question itself: 'One should not talk for long time when sitting in the company because ... ' Similarly in Line 10 for the question, 'What is the main weakness of "long talkers" and how should it be dealt with?', she starts the answer thus: 'The main weakness of long talkers is that ... '

The main interactional pattern in the classes of both Mrs Renu Chopra and Mrs Dhingra is whole class lecture in a teacher-fronted class. Though the students do ask a few questions now and again, on the whole they sit quietly and take notes or just listen. In both Transcripts 2 and 3 there is no student talk at all. The video of Transcript 2 shows that children are listening with rapt attention poring over their books. Mrs Dhingra, like the other teachers in the higher classes, does not face any discipline problems. This pedagogic practice is rooted in the culture of the relationship between students and teachers, which I will discuss in the next section.

Pedagogy and spirituality

'I find my work a divine work.' (Mrs Lalita, 15 March 2005)

The quotation is from the English teacher for Grades 6–10, Mrs Lalita, who is also in charge of the annual cultural festival. Mrs Lalita is a Postgraduate Teacher (PGT), as compared to Mrs Dhingra, who is a Trained Graduate Teacher (TGT). The PGTs teach English to Grades 6–10 and only the TGTs take Classes 11 and 12. Mrs Lalita has been teaching in this RSKV for more than 10 years and knows the students very well.

In an interview (19 December 2006) she elaborated on her statement that her work is divine work. She said, 'Teachers in India have a spiritual bent of mind'. According to Mrs Lalita, all the teachers in the RSKV feel this way. Mrs Lalita does not see her role merely as an English teacher. She says, 'We give them values. We feel connected to the child.' For instance, many of her students share their teenage problems with Lalita. Students come and tell her that 'Ma'am I can't discuss this with my mother but I would like to discuss this with you'.

Another way in which this teacher–student relationship is manifested is the way students behave before the exams. Many will come and touch her feet. Some will say, 'Ma'am I just want to see your face before the exam, then I know that my exam will go well'. Some say, 'please come and see us while we are sitting in the exam then our exam will go well.' Mrs Lalita emphasized that 'They have a deep respect for us'. The students will come and tell her, 'Ma'am we want your wishes before the exam'. Pointing to another teacher, Nisha Singh, who was sitting in the room, Lalitha says that sometimes when Nisha Singh's ex-students are passing by the road they will cross the road and come into the school and touch Nisha Singh's feet in deference to all that she has taught them while they were in the RSKV. At the same time the students also imbibe some, what Mrs. Lalita calls, 'European traditions'. For instance they like to observe 'friendship day'. On this day some of them will come and tie a band around the wrist of the teacher because many of them consider the teacher to be a friend. Mrs Lalita is thus referring to the bicultural personality of the bilinguals in the RSKV.

The issues around culturally situated pedagogy require critical analysis. The literature that supports such pedagogies is extremely valuable. At the same time it is important to keep in mind that the same culturally situated pedagogies can become intractable and immune to pedagogical reform. A case in point is the large-scale intervention in changing interactional patterns undertaken by the World Bank in India (Clark, 2003). Discussing large-scale pedagogical reforms in the District Primary Education Program (DPEP), which covered almost half the districts in India, Clark (2003: 29) comments 'An outcome of the cultural constructedness of teacher thinking and teaching is the embeddedness of practice and its resistance to change'. Clark hypothesizes that four cultural constructs underlie pedagogic practice in India: holism, Karmic duty, hierarchy of relationships, e.g. the guru–shishya relationship, and a view of knowledge that it is accumulated then transmitted. Of these constructs, results of the DPEP show that only holism and conceptions of karmic duty are open to reform.

The drawbacks of culturally situated pedagogies in the RSKV and how some of these might be in need of reform given the changing requirements of English language education in India will be taken up again in Chapter 6, where educational outcomes will be discussed. We now turn to another aspect of the content of biliteracy, namely texts that the students create themselves. These must be seen in tandem with prescribed texts for a more whole picture of textual practices in a biliterate environment.

Creating biliterate and hybrid texts

The photo in Figure 4.2 is from the English text book of a student in Class 10. It shows how the children use their L1 to access the L2. The poem, by William Wordsworth, appears in NCERT (2003c: 32), the English text book for Class 10. The student to whom this text book belongs has underlined all

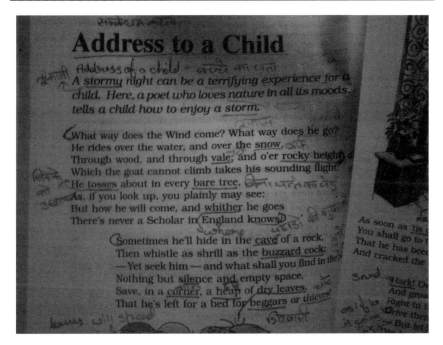

Figure 4.2 Creating a biliterate text in the classroom

the words she has found difficult and written their meanings in Hindi. For instance in the first few lines of the text the following words are glossed:

Stormy: तूफ़ानी
Experience: अनुभव
Terrifying: डरावना

In some cases the student has made annotations in English; for instance she has written 'Address of a child' and glossed this phrase in Hindi as 'बच्चे का पता' so as to make a distinction between the two meanings of the word 'address'. Similarly, in the first line of the poem where Wordsworth says, 'Where does he go?', the student has glossed the pronoun 'he' as 'wind'. This is important as in Hindi nouns have gender and wind is feminine. Here Wordsworth refers to the wind as 'he' with poetic license, even though inanimate objects in English do not have gender. Thus the student felt it necessary to remind herself that the 'he' actually refers to the wind.

The teachers actively encourage the creation of these biliterate annotations in the texts because they use L1 as a resource in the classroom. Mrs Shobhana Gulati explained to me (field notes, 16 October

2005) that the Devanagari script is a great way to teach pronunciation in English. This is because Devanagari is a phonetic script and the words are pronounced exactly the way they are written. There are no silent letters or two pronunciations of a single letter, like /s/ and /k/ for the letter 'c'. Thus if there are difficult pronunciations in the English lesson she makes the children write the exact pronunciation of the English word in Devanagari. Sometimes this mixed media approach does lead to problems. Mrs Gulati mentioned that in the last exam one student in the English test had written her entire paper in Hindi but in the Roman script!

Figure 4.3 shows a recipe that a student, Madhu, in Grade 11, gave me in December 2006. This hybrid text, from the lifeworld of the bilingual, shows how Devanagari and Roman scripts are fused to produce one unified text or a semiotic whole: a recipe. The end product of this recipe itself, a bread roll, is a fusion of Indian and Western cuisines – it is a slice of bread stuffed with spicy potatoes, rolled and deep fried. This is a contextualized artifact as it does not make artificial isoglosses between languages. Thus by encouraging texts like the one shown in 1, the teachers valorize contextualized literacies, shown in Figure 4.3, as a resource in the classroom. At the same time, as the field notes regarding Mrs Shobhana Gulati's comments show, the teachers are aware of the limitations of hybrid

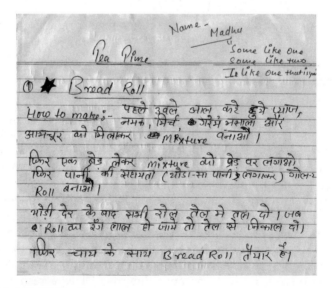

Figure 4.3 A hybrid text

texts in the classroom. For instance, an exam paper, like the one that Mrs. Gulati's student produced, was not acceptable and the student had to re-take the test. Thus the teachers encourage contextualized literacy practices while at the same time they try to supply disadvantaged students with the skills to articulate decontextualized meanings.

Conclusions

This chapter has presented and discussed primary data on the content of biliteracy. Due to the nested nature of the content, contexts, media and development of biliteracy, it is not possible to surgically carve up these territories. Thus in this chapter I have shown how the bilingual program of the RSKV removes the scaffolding of translation as the children acquire competency in English, a concept which also shows the development of biliteracy. Despite this interweaving I have tried to focus on what exactly is taught in the classroom through mainly a discussion of the text books and secondarily through an introduction to student artifacts.

Through culturally sensitive text books that include the urban disadvan-taged, the science text books try to engage the children in a discussion of traditional beliefs versus Western scientific thought. Improvements made in the English text books for primary school have been highlighted; how-ever the chapter shows the dissatisfaction of teachers with the high school English text books. I have shown pedagogic practice in teaching English to the higher classes, which is culturally contextualized in a unique teach-er–student relationship. This relationship is part of the 'guru–shishya' relationship in which the teacher is much more than merely a technicist who disseminates a skill that is necessary for the workplace. Finally this chapter has shown how the children create biliterate texts in the classroom and hybrid texts in their lifeworlds. By valorizing both types of texts the teachers create a link between home and school literacies, encouraging optimal biliterate development.

Chapter 5

In What Contexts is English Taught?

...English can make a man perfect and provide self confidence and make us physically strong and ... We can talk without hesitation. And we can sit amongst all who knows English. ... So English is very good subject for students because in every subject English is must. If we are reading accounts then accounts ... if we are reading Maths then Maths also have English. So first of all we know English then we are able to understand other subjects. So I like English and I want to improve my English. First of all after 12th class I want to get the experience of call centre. So I like English (October 15, 2005).

The statement above is from a female student of grade 12 studying in the RSKV. Many shades of attitudes are apparent herein starting with the feeling that knowledge of the English language can make one confident and 'physically strong'. Since this student studies Accounts and Math in English, she feels she must know English well to understand these subjects. Finally she wants to work in a call centre and thus wants to improve her English. She concludes by remarking that she likes English. This statement not only exhibits instrumental attitudes towards English but also the impression that English is a personality maker, it is knowledge that helps a student process more knowledge and finally it is a subject that students like.

This comment is also an illustration of oracy in English amongst the students of the RSKV. No doubt this text gives the impression that the speaker is not a native speaker of English. Numerous mistakes can be pointed out like article deletion as in 'English is must' which is very common because Hindi does not have articles. However, what I see in this text is fluency of expression and the ability of the student to get her point, regarding the importance of English for her, across.

This chapter is about the contexts in which children become biliterate in India. The continua of biliterate contexts are micro and macro levels of analysis along with competencies along the oral-literate and monolingual-bilingual continua. A micro analysis of interactional patterns in the classroom has been provided in chapters 3 and 4. Here I want to attempt a more macro analysis of attitudes with which students learn English and the goals they have regarding their biliterate competence. Also, I will explore tensions regarding why after 12 years of schooling the students do not have oral competence in English which is a key requirement of the workplace. Thus when the children graduate from the RSKV they are Hindi dominant bilinguals and biliterates without communicative competence in English but good code switching ability and reading competence in English. Their competence in Hindi remains excellent throughout. Thus there is tension between the demands of the globalizing workplace and the English language skills that a school like the RSKV provides.

Data-set for this Chapter

The data set for the book has already been described in the introduction. This chapter is based on a specific subset of that data which needs a detailed description. From December 18 till 31, 2006, I had the good fortune to spend two weeks with the students of grade 12. They had just finished their mid-term exams and there were no regular classes going on in these two weeks. Except for 2 public holidays for Christmas and New Year the children were coming to school on all the other days. As the students were taking extra classes during these two weeks there were a few days when I could not meet them. However I was able to meet the students for 5 days in this two week period for 2 hours per day in which I conducted semi-structured oral and written interviews with the 64 students of grade 12, sections B and C. This essay is based primarily on these 10 hours of oral and written student interviews conducted in December 2006 which make up a subset of my total database of interviews. The oral interviews within these 10 hours are mainly in the form of video files, though some parts are also in form of field notes.

The written interview is based on the following open ended questions that I wrote on the board in English and Hindi. The 64 students answered these questions in class over two weeks.

Is English important for you? Why?
क्या अंग्रेजी आपके लिए ज़रुरी है? क्यों?

Is Hindi important for you? Why?
क्या हिन्दी आपके लिए ज़रुरी है? क्यों?

What are your professional goals?
आपकी अभिलाषाएं क्या हैं?

What role will English play in these professional goals?
इन अभिलाषाओं को प्राप्त करने में अंगरेज़ी का क्या योगदान है?

The students were told to write in their language of comfort and they wrote at length in the both English and Hindi using the Roman and Devanagari scripts. In addition the students were asked to bring artifacts from their daily literacy practices like pages from diaries, recipes, letters to family members and examples of SMSs that they send to their friends. In the oral interviews the students substantiated the answers that they had written down and the artifacts they submitted to me.

This cohort of 64 students I interviewed is extremely homogenous. It consists of all female students in grade 12 of the commerce stream in one school. Nearly all the students are Hindus and come from similar families in terms of household income. All of them have had English for about 12–14 years as one of the media of instruction. As such it is not appropriate to make generalizable claims for the whole of India from this dataset; however, this data is indicative of the attitudes of the urban disadvantaged towards the newly acquired linguistic capital of English.

Instrumental Attitudes Towards English

Table 5.1 Instrumental attitudes towards English

Student No. / translation	Comment
Student 1	People want to speak English only for success in every field they want because it is used in every field & people becomes richie rich by speaking English.
Student 2	In every professional course English is important. In every course English takes its position as a subject also… If you want to do any job English is must there people impress by the people who talk in English. I want to do MBA. In that also English important to communicate with people in that field. Have knowledge about everything in that field.
Student 3 (oral video interview) If we have to go into any profession we should know how to speak English. Like in offices…just like if we go for an interview then if we speak English the people taking our interview will think that he is the best for our company	अगर हमें आगे किसी भी profession में जाना है तो हमें English speaking करना चाहिए…जैसे की offices होते हैं…just like हम interview के लिए जा रहे हैं तो वहां पर जो हमारा interview लेने वाले हैं तो अगर हम English बोलेंगे तो उन्हे लगेगा की he is the best of our company.

Student 4	And I also want to be perfect in speak English because I became to be very Riches person.
Student 5	And in today's time English is must to earn money.

Table 5.2 English Creates a Personality

Student No. /translation	*Comment*
Student 6 I mainly use Hindi but I also give importance to English. When I speak English it feels very good	वैसे मैं ज्यादा हिन्दी का use करती हूं but मैं English को भी importance देती हूं. मैं जब भी English बोलती हूं तो मुझे बहुत अच्छा लगता है...
Student 7 (By speaking and writing English man creates a separate individuality)	English बोलने व लिखने से आदमी की एक अलग पहचान बनती है...
Student 8 (In today's world English is so well known that without English an individual is incomplete)	आज के युग में तो English इस तरह परसिध हो चुकि है कि English के बिना मनुष्य अधूरा है...
Student 9 (oral video interview) (When we speak [English] then the listener likes it. He/she thinks that the speaker is intelligent. Ma'am the one who speaks English will of course be intelligent. I mean the listener gets a different impression. If we speak English they feel positive. They agree with us. If we speak in English they will think that we are truthful...I mean a different impression is created)	जब बोलते हैं तो सुनने वाले को काफ़ी अच्छा लगता है Ma'am उसे यह लगता है कि सामने वाला बहुत intelligent है Ma'am जो English बोलेगा वो ज्यादा intelligent होगा ही. या फिर ज्यादा polish होगी. मतलब सुनने वाले पर अलग effect पड़ता है...अगर हम English बोलते हैं तो उन्हे positive लगता है...हमारी बात को मानते हैं। अगर हम English में बोलेंगे तो उन्हे लगेगा कि हाँ यह सही बोल रहे हैं...मतलब कुछ अलग effect पड़ता है...

Though English is associated with a 'personality' which is imperative for the workplace, Hindi is associated with 'identity' and the religious and cultural traditions of Indians.

Student 14 chose to write about Hindi and English together:

English बहुत तेज़ी से फैल रही है। यह हमारे देश के लिए ज़रुरी भी है परन्तु हिन्दी हमारी नीव हैं और यदि नीव ही मज़बूत नहीं होगी तो हमारा आशियाना कभी भी गिर सकता है...हिन्दी हमारा अस्तित्व है और यदि अस्तित्व ही खो जाए तो हमारा क्या

महत्व...? यदि यह भाषा अस्तित्व में नहीं रही तो हमारी आने वाली पीढ़ी को अपनी राष्ट्रभाषा का ज्ञान नहीं होगा ।

English is spreading fast. It is important for our country but Hindi is our foundation and if our foundation is not strong then our beautiful home may fall. Hindi is our identity, and if we lose this what is our importance? If this language does not remain in our identity then our future generations will not know their national language

The students were very keen to share artifacts from their daily literacy practices with me. The following is an illustration of SMSs that the students send to each other:

Har Khushee Ko Teri Taraf Mode Duo
Tere liye Chand-Taare Tak Tode Duo
Khushiyon Ke Darwaje Tere Liye Khol Duo
Itna Kafi Hai Ya 2–4 Zhoth Aur Bol Duo

(All happiness I turn towards you
The moon and stars I pluck for you
The doors of happiness I open for you
If this is not enough then I can tell 2–4 more lies for you)

Discussion

Hindi: a problematic solidarity

The impression that Hindi is a national language that binds all Indians is controversial. As I have shown in Chapter 1, Table 1.2, according to the 1991 census only about 40% of Indians speak Hindi. However, though Hindi is not spoken by the majority in India, it is the most widely spoken language in the city of Delhi. Thus for Student 13 in Table 5.3 to think that "हिन्दी हमारे देश की पहचान है।" (Hindi is the mark of our country) and that "सभी भारतवासियों की पहचान हिन्दी है।" (Hindi is the mark of all Indians) is demographically incorrect. Student 12 in the same table thinks that "हिन्दी हमें हमारे देश से जोड .ती है।" meaning "Hindi joins us to our country." However this is not borne out by the fact that 60% of Indians are non-Hindi speakers and most of them do not understand any Hindi.

Student 19 in Table 5.4 acknowledges the diversity of India by commenting that there are numerous castes and religions in India. However what she lists, "जैसे बंगाली, मद्रासी, मुस्लिम", meaning "Like Bengali, Madrasi, Muslim" are two linguistic groups and one religious group. Student 19 does not mention a caste name at all. She then writes "इस कारण वश भी हिन्दी का महत्व ज्यादा है" implying that it is Hindi that binds these diverse

Table 5.3 Hindi and Identity

Student No./translation	*Comment*
Student 10 (In our life Hindi has special importance because we are 'Hindustaani'. And we are proud of being 'Hindustaani'.)	हमारे जीवन में हिन्दी भाषा का एक विशिष्ट महत्व है क्योंकि हम एक हिन्दुस्तानी हैं और हमें हिन्दुस्तानी होने का गर्व है.
Student 11 (Hindi is our national language thus it has more importance. It is this Hindi that is a mark of our being Indian)	हिन्दी हमारी राष्ट्र भाषा होने के कारण अधिक महत्व रखती है. यही हिन्दी भाषा हमारे भारतीय होने की निशानी है ...
Student 12 (Hindi is our national language. Hindi joins us to our country)	हिन्दी language हमारी राष्ट्रीय भाषा है. हिन्दी हमें हमारे देश से जोड .ती है।
Student 13 (Hindi is one of the mother tongues of our country. Hindi is the markof our country. In our country Hindi is very important because it is the mark of all Indians)	हिन्दी हमारे देश की एक मात्रभाषा है। हिन्दी हमारे देश की पहचान है। हमारे देश में हिन्दी बहुत जरुरी है क्योंकि सभी भारतवासियों की पहचान हिन्दी है।

linguistic and religious groups together. That the state of Tamil Nadu (Madras is the capital of the state of Tamil Nadu. Student 19 is referring to the Tamils when she writes 'Madrasi'.) actively opposed the officialization of Hindi, which is one of the reasons why English was chosen as a co-official language, draws attention to the misconceptions of seeing Hindi as a national language

The positionality of Hindi as a national language and its ability to build solidarity through language planning is contested from the time of India's independence in 1947. Language planners in India were influenced by the ex-Soviet Union and the status of Russian in the ex-Soviet Union was given to Hindi in India (Schiffman, 1996). However Hindi was never accepted by non-Hindi speakers who feared disenfranchisement, especially in employment opportunities in government offices which would favor Hindi speakers. In 1965 when Hindi was to become the sole official and national language of India, there were linguistic riots in the southern state of Tamil Nadu in protest of this language policy. The situation had become so volatile that Jawaharlal Nehru, then Prime Minister of India, resorted to keeping both English and Hindi as co-official languages.

Table 5.4 Hindi's link with religion and culture

Name/translation	Comment
Student 15 Hindi is very important for us be-cause it is our national language our Vedas our (illegible) are all connected with this language	हिन्दी हमारे लिए बहुत महत्वपूर्ण है क्योंकि यह हमारी राष्ट्रीय भाषा है हमारे वेद हमारे ---- सब इसी भाषा से जुड़े हुए हैं
Student 16	Our prayer, Vedas, Geeta, Ramayana are written in Hindi and Sanskrit also. So to read them we have to know Hindi language
Student 17 Hindi is a legacy/gift of our ancestors this we should not forget	हिन्दी हमारे पूर्वजों की देन है हमें यह नहीं भूलना चाहिए
Student 18	Hindi is an important language be-cause it is our cultural language
Student 19 In India there are many religions, castes, like Bengalis, Madrasis, Mus-lims for this reason the importance of Hindi is great	भारत मे कइ धर्म, जाति भी हैं, जैसे बंगाली, मद्रासी, मुस्लिम इस कारण वश भी हिन्दी का महत्व ज्यादा है

The Hindu-Hindi link is a prevalent language attitude though it is not borne out by demographic and linguistic data. Referring to South Asia Pandharipande comments that "one of the striking features of the language of religion in this region is that there is no fixed equation of one linguistic form to one religion" (2006:141). That Hinduism is the major-ity religion of India is also reflected in the classroom in this dataset as the majority of the 64 students interviewed are Hindus and only one, Rehnuma, is Muslim. Student 16 in Table 5.4 comments: "Our prayer, Vedas, Gita, Ramayana are written in Hindi and Sanskrit also. So to read them we have to know Hindi language..." Here the main texts of Hin-duism: the Vedas, the Gita, and the epic Ramayana are associated Hindi though student 16 does know that they are originally written in Sanskrit. Similarly student 15 in Table 5.4 also associates the Vedas with Hindi and lists this as one of the reasons why Hindi is important for her. How-ever Hindu texts have been translated from Sanskrit into all the major languages of India as Hindus speak numerous languages. Student 15's impression of the close relationship between Hindi and Sanskrit is also based on the fact that the two languages share the Devanagari script. However, Sanskrit texts are also available in, for instance, the Bengali and Tamil scripts, thus Sanskrit is accessible to Hindus with literacies in scripts other than Devanagari.

The comments in Table 5.4 confer high status on Hindi by connecting it with Sanskrit, which has retained its prestige in India as the language of Hinduism, and also by linking Hindi with the language of the ancestors of Indians. As such Gal's (1993) concern, that attitudes of status for one language and solidarity for another might not be consistent with the often overlapping and self contradictory impressions of respondents, is borne out by my data. For instance student 17 writes that "हिन्दी हमारे पूर्वजों की देन है" meaning that Hindi is a legacy of our ancestors and thus it is important for us. This impression that Hindi is the language of our ancestors is also founded on the perceived close connection between Hindi and Sanskrit. The notion that Sanskrit is the language of our ancestors is commonplace in India; however, thinking of Hindi in the same way points to the high status that this language has in the ideology of Hindi speakers.

Hegemony of Hindi

The discussion in the previous section also points to the hegemonic reach of Hindi. Hindi speakers think that most Indians speak and/ or understand Hindi. For instance in Table 5.4 student 19 thinks that Hindi is the glue that binds Indians of diverse castes and religions. In the same table student 18 writes that "Hindi is an important language because it is our cultural language", thus implying that Indian culture is a monolithic whole and can be accessed mainly through the Hindi language.

Within the context of Delhi the hegemony of Hindi is powerful. Thus student 20, whose mother tongue is Tamil, is convinced that Hindi is her 'Maatribhasha' or mother tongue. Student 20's survey is given in Figure 5.2.

In the first three sentences of this text, which are in English, student 20 outlines her multilingual competencies. She speaks Hindi, English and Tamil and is biliterate in Hindi and Tamil. Thereafter there is a paragraph mainly in Hindi with some English borrowings. The following is my translation of the full paragraph in Figure 5.2.

> Hindi is important for us because it is our national language. It is important for us to know our nation's language. Because we are born of this soil and being born of this soil if we forget our Hindi language this is shameful for us. The British after living in our country for many years have left their mark within us, that will remain with us, but

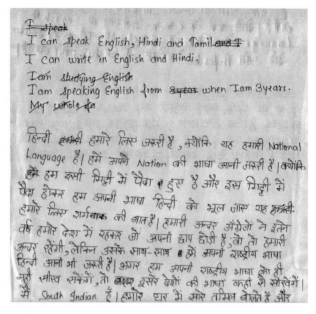

Figure 5.2 Student 20's survey

along with that we must know our national language. If we are not
able to learn our national language, then how will we learn another
country's language. I am a South Indian. In our home we all speak
Tamil and ...

Despite being a South Indian Tamil speaker student 20 is convinced
that Hindi is connected to the soil of India from which she has been born.
In fact she associates the English language with foreignness and a colonial past by mentioning that that is the mark the British have left on us;
however, she does not associate this foreignness with Hindi. Thus though
in the pan-Indian context Hindi faces resistance as a national language,
within the context of Delhi, where it is a dominant language, its hegemonic reach is powerful.

English: not just status

While Hindi is associated with an Indian identity, problematic
though this might be, English is associated with an attractive and successful personality. In Table 5.2 when student 7 writes that "English
बोलने व लिखने से आदमी की एक अलग पहचान बनती है ..." she means that English imparts a distinct individuality to a person. Student 8 comments

that "English के बिना मनुष्य अधूरा है..." meaning that without English an individual is incomplete. Student 9's impression is that an English speaker sounds more intelligent, polished, persuasive and truthful to the listener.

English is associated with becoming rich and with attaining higher education leading to a good job. In Table 5.1, which is about instrumental attitudes towards English, students 1, 4 and 5 link English with money. Though student 1 seems to have a low opinion of people who want to become 'richie rich' by speaking English, student 5's comment pragmatically states that "English is must to earn money". Student 4 is openly ambitious and pragmatic saying that she wants to perfect her English because she wants to become rich. Though tertiary education in India is available in Hindi, the young women are aware that the road to changing their social class must pass through higher education in English. Thus student 2, who wants to do an MBA, thinks that English is important for her. She feels that not only will people in her workplace be impressed if she speaks English, the language will also give her access to "knowledge about everything in that field".

That English develops a personality and Hindi an identity is a distinction made by these students. When I was coding the data from these interviews the words/phrases that the students repeatedly used in relation to Hindi were: अस्तित्व (identity), नींव (foundation), मातृभाषा (Sanskrit for mother tongue), राष्ट्रभाषा (Sanskrit for national language), देश की पहचान (mark of the country), and मिट्टी (soil). The use of these emotional words and phrases show a language ideology in which Hindi is the fundamental link with the country and Indianness. In contrast the codes that came up for English were: job, rich/money, विकास (development of individual and country), उन्नति (progress), अलग पहचान (unique look), impressed (as in the listener is impressed if the speaker speaks English). These codes imply that English is restricted to superficial trappings at the level of a social and workplace personality though these trappings are considered essential for success. The lack of emotional words in association with English implies that it does not touch the soul of the respondents as does Hindi.

Though the parents of these students are involved in manual jobs, as described under 'Site and Data Collection', the young women of the RSKV have high ambitions. As their choice of profession they listed: accountant, fashion designer, air hostess, teacher, business woman, Managing Director in a multi national company, member of an NGO (Non Governmental Organization) and a member of the Indian Administrative Service. They wrote that English is essential for all these professions and that this is one of the reasons they like studying English.

Though English is not a common mode of communication amongst the children in speech, their literacy practices show that it is not only used in SMSs but also to write personal diaries which others do not usually read, and to write recipes. On p. 80 I have shown an SMS joke that one of the students had recently sent to a friend. This is a biliterate-hybrid text type where Hindi, which is usually written in the Devanagari script, is written on a mobile phone in the Roman script in transliterated form. As of now there are no mobile phones in the Indian market in which the Devanagari script can be used. Thus though most 'Dilliwalahs' (residents of Delhi) have phones, only those with literacy in English can send SMSs.

The hybrid text type shown in the SMS is an illustrations from the daily literacy practices and language choices of the young women in which English is not confined to the domain of school and, by extension, the workplace. Similarly the e-mail shown on p. 38 and Figure 4.3 on p. 74 are hybrid texts written in both English and Hindi using the Devanagari and Roman scripts in one composite text. These texts show a mingling of scripts and can commonly be seen in advertisements, billboards, posters and other artifacts in the multilingual ecology of Delhi. Creating such texts makes these young girls feel trendy, fun loving and imaginative, which is precisely the message of such advertisements. Thus the bilingual students of the RSKV use their competencies creatively to disseminate texts for enjoyment and communication in which English is an integral part of their personality.

Figure 5.1, a monoliterate text, shows that English is the language of choice for writing a personal diary for some of these young women. This student was willing to share a page of her diary with me though she usually does not like showing this text to anyone. She said she likes to write her diary in English not only because it is good practice for her but because she likes English as a subject and enjoys using the language to communicate with herself. These literacy practices indicate that the students of the RSKV do not view English merely as an instrumental tool for professional and monetary gain. Rather English is part of the personal lives of these young women for communication with themselves and their friends, and also for creating biliterate-hybrid texts which are enjoyable to write.

Tensions Between Educational Goals and Outcomes

In various interviews with students I have been told that the girls are very happy with the English that they have learned in school. However

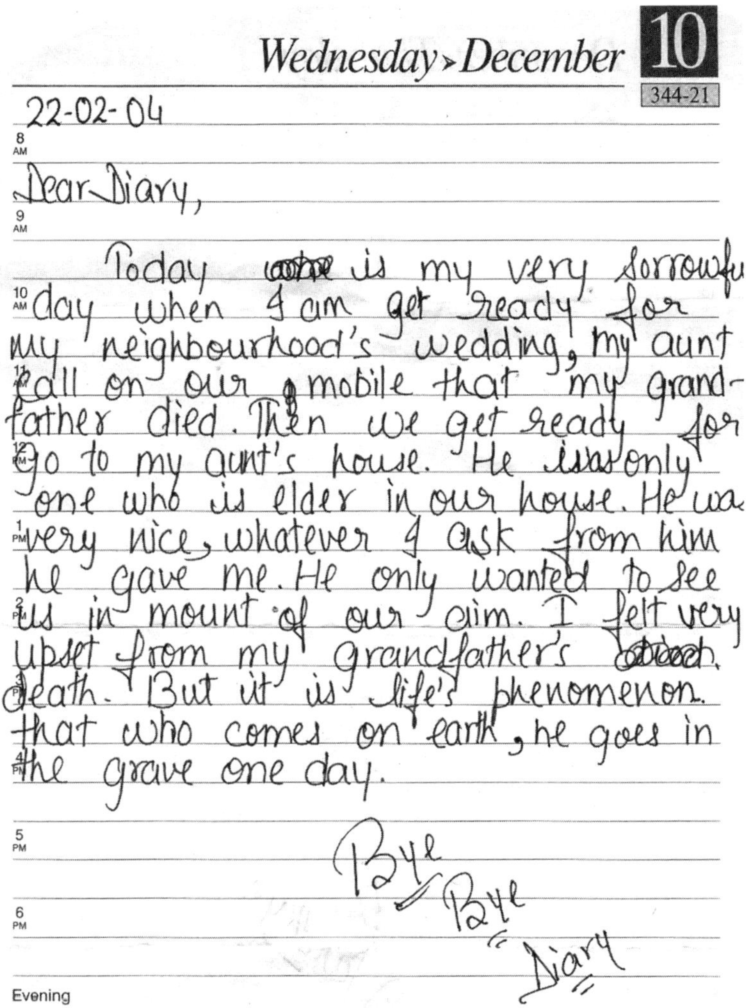

Figure 5.1 Page from personal diary

their concern is that they cannot speak in English. For instance Sweta Tomar a student of grade five reported that she has learned a lot of English with her teacher, Priya Ma'am. Sweta likes to write 10 sentence compositions on topics like 'My vacation' and can write all the 10 sentences on her own without copying. However, Sweta was not able to have a simple conversation with me in English. Though she would start a sentence quite confidently, she would break down quickly and revert to talking animatedly in Hindi.

Mrs. Charu, the high school English teacher, thinks that though the school has not equipped students with enough communicative competence for the workplace, many of the graduates take an English speaking course after school and improve. Thus Mrs. Charu asserts that schools like the RSKV do provide the necessary and sufficient conditions on the basis of which the students can learn communicative English from service providers outside of the school system. In this sense, and because schools like the RSKV are offering English from nursery itself, Mrs. Charu believes there is some improvement towards equitable access to linguistic capital (October 17, 2006). The problem is that communicative English is then learned only outside school in the open linguistic market where there are many providers of such commodified packages: e.g. Rapidex English Speaking Course.

A graduate of the RSKV, Vimla, has taken such an English speaking course. Vimla's father, who earns less than Rupees 5000 per month (USD 50), is a cook in an Army Officers Mess. Her mother, a homemaker, has not had formal schooling. When Vimla graduated from school in 2003 she immediately joined The British School of Language in South Extension, New Delhi. This was a 3 month course and she joined to improve her spoken English. In The British School of Language they started with grammar, went on to vocabulary and then taught spoken English through topic based group discussions. She reports that she not only enjoyed the course but also improved tremendously while taking the course. However, after the course she regressed and experienced loss of communicative ability as she did not have the opportunity to use what she had learned in her immediate environment.

The course cost Rupees 2500 which Vimla saved from the online marketing job that she has on weekends. To get this online marketing job Vimla first had to take a computer course. Vimla reports that the English she has learned in her school is adequate because during this Aptec computer course she did not have any problem understanding the content of the computer class which was mainly in English though the instructor also used Hindi when necessary. Vimla's income is currently nearly double that of her father. She not only helps with the expenses of their house but also bears the cost of educating her three younger siblings (field notes, March 28, 29, 2005).

In various interviews the teachers in the RSKV have commented that the main reason why their students are not able to acquire communicative competence in English is because it is confined to the domain of school and later the workplace; they do not use English in any other domain like family and friends or religion. There is no immersive environment for them in which to learn English. Even in the domain of media the dominant language is Hindi though, as I have shown in this chapter, the children do SMS in the Roman script and a few write diaries.

Some teachers like Lalita actively try to impart speaking skills in English. In an interview Lalita commented that speaking in English is very much part of her personal curriculum. In her high school English classes she starts the week with a speech. She gives the students the topic for the speech earlier; the topics could be like 'truth' 'discipline' or 'love'. Lalita's students take this part of the class very seriously. Many of the students prepare extensively if it is their turn to make a speech and become an inspiration for the rest of the class. Lalita is aware that making a speech is not like a conversation; however, she finds that this kind of speech event works very well in her classroom and the students enjoy the opportunity to use the language that they have learned in their English classes. In this speech event Lalita does not correct their mistakes but lets them express themselves. Lalita remarks that some of her students are able to have a conversation in English though they might not be able to sustain this for very long (field notes, December 19, 2006).

Conclusions

Indian students have positive attitudes towards both Hindi and English. They associate English with an international language the knowledge of which will lead them to a good job. It will develop their personality, make them confident and strong and give others a good impression of them. English can make them appear reliable and truthful. At the same time English is also an inherent part of their daily literacy practices and thus a part of their identity though they tend to associate English with 'personality' rather than 'identity'.

On the other hand Hindi is associated with being a 'national language', with being Indian and being Hindu, though demographic and linguistic data do not really justify these impressions. Most of the students have the impression that the Hindi language is common to all Indians and is what makes them Indian. These attitudes towards Hindi and English point to a hyphenated identity: an individual who thinks of herself as nationally rooted but confident, ambitious, intelligent and prepared for the globalizing workforce of a modernizing India. All the students surveyed are ambitious for their future and do not see themselves doing the same jobs as their parents. They are aware that the linguistic capital of English has a high degree of convertibility in the employment market and are anxious to make good use of what they have learned in school.

Though English is largely associated with status and Hindi with solidarity, this dichotomy is problemetized in this chapter in light of the responses of the students. Their responses show many of the misconceptions of the linguistic majority, which is what Hindi speakers are in India, regarding how pervasive their language is throughout the country and how representative it is of Indians or Hindus. As such attitudes towards Hindi show the overconfidence and insularity of Hindi speakers towards their language and how it fits into the linguistic ecology of India.

This chapter has shown a tension between educational goals and outcomes. In terms of the continua of biliterate contexts the students are progressing towards the bilingual end of the monolingual-bilingual continuum. Cuturally situated pedagogies are well suited to the background of the students in the RSKV. However they face many problems in this journey. Though English is primarily a language for instrumental purposes for the urban disadvantaged and schools like the RSKV strive to provide workplace skills through the English language curriculum, this is not the outcome. Graduates of the RSKV do not have the communicative competence in English which the globalizing workplace requires. However the school does produce Hindi dominant bilinguals with emergent competencies in biliteracy. Like Vimla, some of the graduating students take speaking courses in English and thus complement their workplace skills with what the school has provided. Thus there is a space for pedagogical reform through which communicative competence in English can be provided within the 12 years of schooling itself.

Chapter 6
How Much is Learned?

Hornberger's (2003) continua of biliterate development may be interpreted as a documentation, both qualitative and quantitative, of how much is learned at various key stages as the learner becomes biliterate. Related to this is the value of biliteracy for the individual in terms of what biliteracy will be used for. For the purposes of this study, a key stage is when the student graduates after 12 years of schooling. In the case of English language education in India, despite the fact that the children do use English for other than instrumental functions, the prevailing attitude towards English is still that it is learned because it is a requirement of the workplace. Thus I consider it important to explore a workplace which is an illustration of a globalizing India and where young 'agents' use their biliterate skills to make a living.

This chapter, consequently, is about a call center. I start with a brief review of the literature on literacy and the workplace, which has relevance for a developing country like India. I go on to explore the expectations of the workplace in terms of the linguistic resources that young 'agents' bring with them. My attempt in this section of the book is to present a close look at the bilingual and biliterate practices of this workplace with an eye on how government-sponsored bilingual education in India is preparing students for this new employment sector. The previous chapters would have given the reader an idea of how well or not government schools like the RSKV have prepared their students for meeting these requirements. In keeping with the points on the continua of biliterate development, I keep my analysis around reception–production, oral–written and L1–L2.

Sarvodaya: Welfare for All

The relationship of work and employment opportunity with schooling is important in a developing country where the unemployment rate is very high. As mentioned earlier in this book, the word 'Sarvodaya' in the name of the RSKV is a concept from the work of the social thinker Mohandas Karamchand Gandhi (1869–1948). Gandhi, with his loincloth, bare wiry body and staff, is the ultimate symbol of the subaltern, the disadvantaged, the have-not. Though a successful lawyer by profession from a middle-class family, Gandhi carefully cultivated this 'politics of dress' to constantly remind his audience about the poor. His idea of, सर्वोदय or 'Sarvodaya', meaning universal welfare, is drawn from John Ruskin (1819–1900), who was an extremely well known art critic, poet and social theorist of his time. Gandhi's (1955) book, *Sarvodaya*, is a paraphrase of John Ruskin's (1985) *Unto This Last*, a set of four essays that Ruskin published in 1860. *Unto This Last* is a set of essays on political economy, particularly about how uncontrolled industrialization is the root cause of abject poverty in the UK.

Gandhi defined Sarvodaya as, 'सच्चे लोकतंत्र का सपना', or the dream of a truly egalitarian society. In this society there would be equality between lawyer and barber, the latter being the lowest of the low castes, as each had the same rights and status in society. Though this may seem a commonplace statement today, in the India of the late 19th century, to give an Untouchable the same status as a lawyer was an idea that rocked the foundations of a caste-based society.

Gandhi envisions:

ऐसा समाज ... जीवन मिनार की शकल में नहीं होगा, जहाँ ऊपर की तंग चोटी को नीचे के चौड़े पाये पर खड़ा रहना पड़ता है । वहाँ तो जीवन समुद्र की लहरों की तरह एक के बाद एक घेरे की शकल में होगा, जिसका केन्द्र व्यक्ती होगा ।

Such a society …will not be in the shape of a tower, where the narrow summit rests on a broad base. There life will be in the form of ripples, and the center: the individual.

This quotation shows that Gandhi was trying to change a class- and caste-based society where a few controlled the millions. It also shows the spiritual capital that Gandhi valued. It was on the basis of the spirituality and character of the individual that he founded the idea of Sarvodaya. Throughout the book he emphasizes that truth, non-violence and character are the bases of a new society.

Gandhi's model of national education is based on a vocation or life skill, leading to self-sufficiency, the mother tongue as medium of education and character building. He implemented this educational system on rural communes he set up like the Tolstoy farm started in 1910 in Johannesburg and the Phoenix ashram started in 1904, which was located near Durban, South Africa. He writes:

सारी शिक्षा किसी दस्तकारी या उद्योग के द्वारा दी जाय

All education should be imparted through a handicraft or industry. (Gandhiji, 1955: 156)

The rationale for this is:

इस प्रकार की शिक्षा-पद्धती में मस्तिष्क और आत्मा का उच्चतम विकास समभव है ।

In this type of educational model the brain and the soul can attain the highest development.

Regarding the media of education, Gandhi wrote in Harijan on 25 August 1946:

मेरा मानना है कि अंग्रेजी शिक्षा ने हमारे दिमागों को कंगाल बना दिया है,...और उन्हे साहसी नागरिकता के लिये कभी तैयार नहीं किया ।

It is my belief that English education has bankrupted our minds... and has left us unprepared for courageous citizenship. (Prabhu & Rao, 2003: 364)

Further in the same entry he comments:

मातृभाषा मनुष्य के मानसिक विकास के लिये उसी प्रकार स्वाभाविक है जिस प्रकार माँ का दूध शिशु के शरीर के लिये

The mother tongue is as natural for the mental development of man as mother's milk is for the baby. (Prabhu & Rao, 2003: 368)

The bilingual program of the Sarvodaya Schools has some differences from the rules laid down by Gandhi though it by and large follows the essence of Sarvodaya. For instance all Sarvodayas do not have a vocational wing, unlike the Sarvodaya School in Delhi Cantonment, and the learning of a handicraft or trade is not the basis of education in many of the Sarvodayas. During Gandhi's lifetime itself there were concerns that this model could become a screen for the malpractice of child labor. However, I see the teaching of English as a vocational skill directly related to making the children self-sufficient.

Also, according to the Kothari Commission Report of 1964–65, secondary schooling in India is supposed to be vocationalized. The Sarvodaya schools service some of the poorest in urban India and give them access to the linguistic capital of English, which, before the 1990s, was the fiefdom of the upper middle classes. At the same time, through the Three Language Formula, the RSKVs are also imparting the spiritual capital Gandhi was concerned about. In this sense the schools are living up to Gandhi's dream of an egalitarian new society.

India Calling: The Call Center

There have been some excellent accounts of activity in call centers, also called Business Processes Outsourcing (BPOs) in India, from the point of view of journalism (Friedman, 2005). There is also an emergent literature on the call center as a site for exploring the multilingual workplace. For instance Roy (2003) has done extensive research on French–English bilinguals in a Canadian call center. She finds that this new employment sector valorizes the linguistic capital of the Francophone community. At the same time the call center demands standardized French and English that devalues the local French dialect of the community.

Similarly Cameron's (2000) research site is also a call center, though she looks at call centers located in the UK and Scotland, where the language used is exclusively English. Cameron's focus is on the use of feminized language that the call center encourages. An important point that Cameron makes concerns the 'style' of language and identity adopted by the phone operators. She writes that, unlike the adolescents in the Rampton (1995) study, who are 'crossing' into other identities of their own volition, here the phone operators are doing so because the supervisors and the workplace demands it. Both Cameron (2000) and Roy (2003) seem to have a negative view of language standardization measures adopted in call centers. Their work suggests that this is an imposition on the linguistic identity of the individual, which I don't share.

Linguistic skills for the globalizing workplace

I had the opportunity to visit the XYZ call center in a posh part of Delhi. The marketing officer, Arbaaz, invited me to the center at 6.30 p.m., as call centers in India are active only at night when customers in the US and Europe are awake. The building from inside seemed exactly like a small corporation in the USA. Arbaaz, a 30-something Muslim, took me to the 'floor', where row after row of agents, most of them young adults in jeans and sweaters, were seated at computers talking on the phone.

One of them was dealing with a collections call. Arbaaz gave me a set of headphones and I could hear both the agent and her American customer at the other end. The agent who had made this call was persuading the American to make a US$135 payment on his credit card, as he had defaulted on previous payments. Arbaaz explained to me that this kind of collections call is one of their main businesses. The young female agent said, 'Can you make this payment by Friday?' She said 'Friday' very much like an American, exaggerating the 'ah' after 'Fr'.

The point person for hiring, Radhika, at XYZ call center, described in detail the linguistic capital they expect the employees to bring with them and also how the call center hones the same through training:

> We assess them on sentence construction, grammar, accent, rate of speech and fatal disqualifiers. Aahs and oohs. Whatever like ah ah I did this and I all that you know. We look at the …Because while speaking to the customer if you are making such noise its not right. (27 December 2005)

Radhika explains that if employees have a strong mother tongue influence (MTI), they are not considered to be an appropriate 'voice profile' and might be given a back office job. The others are trained in accent neutralization. They are taught American pronunciation like how to say in-ven-to-ry with the stress on the third syllable. This is a challenge for Hindi speakers because Hindi, like most other Indian languages, does not have syllabic stress and it takes a long time for Indians to put their foot on the correct syllable. In grammar training the employees are taught to speak in short sentences at a slow pace. For instance, for some processes the agent should speak at a rate of 10 words per minute, with pauses for the customer to process what the agent is saying, and with an accuracy of about 85%.

In the following section of the interview, an integral part of the training process is described. The conversation is between Arbaaz from the marketing department, Radhika from Human Resource and the author.

Transcript 1

Radhika: हाँ. Accent neutralization कह लो. You are removing MTIs. Also we teach them the ability to understand …listening skills are very important. The first day I took a call I said 'what the hell he's speaking!'

Viniti: This was a American client?

Radhika: This was a Britisher. तो Britisher तो फिर भी समझ में आ जाता है …

Radhika: *This was a Britisher. So a Britisher can still be understood…*

Arbaaz: Like the Britishers also have about 50–60 types of accents. So they have to understand…We have in-house trainers. We do a lot of things actually. We have culture. That's very

	important. We have people who actually sit and research the culture. We have a team that just researches the client. And researches the culture. Those are the cultural modules.
Radhika:	How do they eat. How do they ...er What do they like?
Arbaaz:	If they have to make a conversation with the guy ...
Radhika:	You know he's waiting and ....means what do you like .... because he could spend 20–25 minutes on the call. Yeah again depending on process to process. And you are assessing की इसको कितना पैसा देना है. So you need to assess that. तो वो wait कर रहा है. So you have to make polite conversation.
Arbaaz:	Cultural means that you give an understanding ... All kinds of things film stars. Famous cities... (27 December 2005)

Transcript 1 shows that, as reported in the work of Cameron (2000) and Roy (2003), in this call center there is a process of language standardization going on along with the making of a new workplace identity. Radhika emphasizes accent neutralization, which means correcting MTI. She also emphasizes listening skills, as the agents must be able to decode various types of British and American accents. As some calls can take up to 45 minutes, the agents are taught the culture of the client as a separate module so that they can talk about the client's cities, movie stars and food. Such a conversation can be a challenge for agents, as none of them can afford to visit cities in the UK and USA, although they are exposed to Western culture through Hollywood movies dubbed in Hindi.

English language training in a call center

Tulika Chopra, an Indian brought up in the UK, is in charge of English language training in XYZ call center (fieldnotes, 30 December 2006). Tulika says that most of the candidates who apply for an agent's job come from government schools. For instance many are from the Kendriya Vidyalayas. Though these children do not speak English at home or with their friends, they have studied English for 12 years. As such this sociolinguistic profile fits exactly with the students I have been observing in the RSKV. After school most of them take an English-speaking course. Some of the courses are the '15 din mein English bolna seekhiye' or 'learn English in 15 days' type of commodified packages, which are inexpensive and very readily available in the urban linguistic market. Some students take the Rapidex English speaking course, which Tulika thinks is better. Despite these shortcomings Tulika comments that many of these students have an excellent vocabulary. The problem is that when they try to speak English they translate from Hindi; they don't think in English (fieldnotes, 30 December 2006). We can see here a tension between the pedagogies of the RSKV, specifically the 'indirect method' of Mrs Dhigra, which is based on translation, and the requirements of the workplace.

Tulika gets a lot of candidates from Postal Code 6 in Delhi, which is the Old Delhi area. These children come from extremely disadvantaged families. For instance Tulika interviewed a candidate whose father was a chowkidaar, or a security guard hired by the government to patrol the streets in the night with a long staff. Tulika thinks that in a way these children are gifted because they have excellent customer service skills. She adds, 'I don't mean they have a servile attitude'; on the other hand, what she is referring to is a pleasant manner in tone, which is very important while doing business on the phone. They have some computer training. She thinks of this cohort as good students and well suited for a job in a call center. She also gets a lot of students from the neighboring city of Lukhnow. One of the problems with candidates from Lukhnow is that they never get over saying 'Estation' for 'station'. This is one of the characteristics of the regional accent in which the speaker tends to add 'a' before a syllable that begins with 's'.

In the first instance Tulika speaks to new candidates on the phone. Only if she feels confident about the student's skills in English oracy does she ask them to come in for a face-to-face interview. In this telephonic conversation the candidates often repeat prepared sentences, thus Tulika does not take this as their real ability in English. In the face-to-face interview she tries to have a conversation in English. For instance she asks 'What did you do on the weekend?' and usually gets a response like 'I went to movie', which indicates to her that these are not really English speakers.

Appendix 2 shows the structure of a 15-day training program done at XYZ call center called Foundations of Voice Training, after which the agents are 'on the floor', which means they begin to take calls on the job. In this training schedule Unit 3 on Day 1 is about accent reduction, which I have shown is an important concern of the management at XYZ. Day 2, Unit 1 is about rate of speech, which is essential for agents from India, as Indians tend to speak very fast. The subsequent units show an emphasis on phonetics and correct pronunciation of vowels and consonants. The whole of Day 4 is devoted to stress and rhythm. This is extremely important for speakers of Hindi and other Indian languages, as Indians tend to put their foot squarely on a different syllable. For instance the word '**in**dustry' is usually pronounced in the UK and USA with the stress on the first syllable, but in India the stress is usually on the second one as in 'in**du**stry'.

On the whole this training program can work for many of the graduates of the RSKV whom I have interviewed and showcased in this book. Tulika herself points out that many of her recruits are from government schools who have taken a speaking course after school, confirming that bilingual education in government schools does provide the necessary and sufficient skills with which the students can be trained for the globalizing workplace. Thus with regards to the continua of biliterate development, the necessary and sufficient skills are learned. However a lot more needs to be done in terms of changing interactional patterns in the classroom, teacher training and curriculum development to include communicative competence as an outcome of English-medium schooling in government schools.

Call center agents and their agency

Deepika and her sister Ranjana both work in this call center. They graduated from Guru Teg Bahadur Public School in Meerut, which is a small town a few hours' drive from Delhi. As my mother's family is also from Meerut, I know this town quite well. Though Guru Teg Bahadur is a Public School, the quality of education in this school is comparable to that of the RSKV in Delhi. Deepika is wearing jeans and a sweater, whereas Ranjana is in a salwar kameez. Both the sisters are in their early 20s.

Satish, who also works as an agent in this call center, is from the North-eastern state of Nagaland. His mongoloid features and fair skin make him look Chinese, which is the racial type of Indians from the North-eastern states. He graduated from the Kohima school, a private English-medium school. Satish says that he is also a small town boy. The college he went to, St. Joseph's, 'was in the middle of a big jungle, you know', he jokes, referring to the forested terrain of the state of Nagaland. He is wearing jeans with numerous pockets on the sides and a sweatshirt with a hood. He is also a 20-something.

Deepika, Ranjana and Satish bring rich linguistic resources to their workplace. The two sisters speak English and Punjabi at home because, as Deepika says, 'We are Punjabis'. In school Deepika studied English, Punjabi and Sanskrit, whereas Ranjana studied English and Punjabi. The two sisters are also fluent speakers of Hindi, because that is the main language of Delhi and they have been living and working here for many years. Satish's home languages are Nagamese and English. However, he too can converse with his friends in Hindi, as he has been in Delhi since the year 2000.

Deepika and Ranjana mention that when they are off work and the person next to them speaks Hindi or Punjabi, that is the language they prefer to use because, as Deepika says, 'It makes us feel close'. Satish's language of comfort is Nagamese, but no one in Delhi speaks this language, so he uses it only when he goes home. With his friends he uses English or Hindi. When I asked Satish about his identity he said 'I am Indian first and then Naga'. Ranjana, like Deepika, also values her Punjabi identity. She is highly biliterate in Gurmukhi (the script of Punjabi) and reads voraciously. The sisters feel they are Punjabi and Indian.

In Transcript 1, where Radhika and Arbaaz describe the training process of the agents, there is no doubt that a certain linguistic identity is being imposed on the employee. It is an identity in which there is no MTI, there is accent neutralization and the resulting product is a 'voice profile' that is pleasing to the customer and can persuade a defaulting American customer to make a payment. It is also an identity in which agents can talk knowledgeably about cities in the USA and the UK although they have never visited these cities. The agents talk about the food, customs, movie stars and culture of the customers from the USA and UK as if they know it very well.

This identity has been problematized by Shome (2006). She finds that studies of diaspora and hybridity must move away from North Atlantic geographical spaces and enter Asian geographies because there are new modernities at issue here that have not been dealt with by diaspora studies. Specifically, diaspora studies have concentrated on the third world subject leaving home for the first world and the implications for a hybrid identity that this 'arrival' entails. However, call center workers are not leaving India, yet they enter a different enunciative space when they are at work which is their 'American' identity. Shome sees this as aural racism as compared to the racism of the body; it is racism through control of voice, accent, rate of speech and knowledge of the culture of the client.

I could not disagree more. In view of a hybrid Indian identity, which is a syncretic pastiche of multiple linguistic identities, the agent in the call center does not see anything particularly negative in putting on a work voice. Deepika, Ranjana and Satish index a cache of identities depending on their sociocultural and sociolinguistic contexts. This could be a Punjabi- or English-speaking identity for Deepika and Ranjana. It could be a Nagamese- or English- or Hindi-speaking identity for Satish. Similarly there is a workplace identity, and because it is language work that these agents do, they put on a linguistic identity to do their work well. According to Gee *et al.* (1996: xiv), '...The new work order is largely about trying to create new social identities or new kinds of people...', and this is exactly what Deepika, Ranjana and Satish invent and imagine when they are on the floor.

The hybrid identities of Ranjana, Deepika and Satish are not the same as the new identities discussed by Rampton (1995). Rampton describes the use of Punjabi by Anglo- and Afro-Caribbean adolescents. However their knowledge of Punjabi is limited to swear words, terms of deprecation and a selection of stock formulae. Rampton reports that Indian and Pakistani youth welcome such crossings from their white and black friends and see this as an attempt at inter-racial friendships. He calls this 'crossing'; however I believe such crossing is not only superficial but also unsustainable because the crossers do not know the language into which they are crossing. An illustration of the unsustainability of such a relationship is manifested in the way that Afro-Caribbean adolescents reacted to Bhangra music. Rampton emphasizes that Bhangra music, which originated in the Punjab, is something that Anglo- and Afro-Caribbean adolescents encountered in the youth clubs. However, they did not show active interest in this music, unlike their Indian and Pakistani friends. The bilingual adults I have presented in this chapter know English well as a workplace language. Like the students of the RSKV, they read and write in English and participate in those cultural activities that they can afford, like watching Hollywood movies. Thus I see the identities of Dev, Ranjana, Deepika and Satish as a hybrid pastiche rather than simply 'crossing'.

Breaking the Bourdieusian चक्रव्यूह (Chakravyuh)

The Sanskrit word चक्रव्यूह (Chakravyuh) is from the Hindu epic the Mahabharata. It refers to a circular impenetrable formation in war created by the enemy. During the war of the Mahabharata, which was fought between two factions of the same family, the young Abhimanyu was caught inside the चक्रव्यूह (Chakravuyh) of the Kaurava faction. Though he fought valiantly, and in the end he only had the broken wheel of his chariot to defend himself, he could not break the चक्रव्यूह (Chakravuyh) and died struggling inside it.

I see the chains of caste and class in India as a चक्रव्यूह (Chakravuyh) encircling the urban disadvantaged. In Bourdieusian terms this is the idea of social reproduction, which means that the children of one income group remain for generations in that income group and are unable to break out of their poverty. Bourdieu and Passeron write:

> …In the last proposition (4.3) do we expressly characterize the school PA which reproduces the dominant culture, contributing thereby to the reproduction of the structure of the power relations within a social

formation in which the dominant system of education tends to secure a monopoly of legitimate symbolic violence. (Bourdieu & Passeron, 1977: 6)

The authors are saying that pedagogic action (PA) in national school systems valorizes only the dominant culture of a society and thus the school system reproduces class divisions. This is exactly what the RSKV is trying not to do. It is trying not to reproduce the dominant culture, of only middle-class Indians having access to the linguistic capital of English, by providing linguistic capital to the urban disadvantaged. Thus I see this PA in the RSKV not as symbolic violence but, on the contrary, this PA is in keeping with the Gandhian ideal of श्रम (Shram) or dignified access to labor. It is important to note that all three agents, Deepika, Ranjana and Satish, are from small towns like Meerut and the remote town of Kohima in North-east India. These 20-somethings have left their families and have come to Delhi to find work and access new employment sectors that are not available to them in their home towns. All of them are using their biliteracy, specifically their knowledge of English, as a vocational skill. As call centers in India function only in the night, both Deepika and Ranjana are doing a night job, which is a significant change in the lifestyle of young women in India.

Gee *et al.* (1996: 22) ask some very important questions regarding school and work. They ask, 'What should the relationship between school and work be? How should schools engage with the new capitalism?'. These are important questions in the context of English language teaching in India because English is primarily used in the domain of the workplace. Radhika, the HR person at the XYZ call center, is aware of this connection between school and work. She says:

> For people from government schools. They need to be groomed. Their grammar has to be good. We do check on the schools because you learn grammar, correct grammar only in your school. So that's the reason we need to stress more on the schools...we need to go down to the teachers and tell them why a call center is good. (27 December 2005)

Radhika is ready to sell this employment sector to the schools as the demand for call center agents in India exceeds the supply. In addition the attrition rate is so high that Radhika is always on the look out for more agents.

Radhika thinks of a call center as a sector that can absorb a lot of the unemployment in India. She says:

This industry is giving you employment ... It's helping the government to resolve unemployment. It's giving you good environment to work in. How many of us make it big. Out of ... So I've been reading in the papers. And people have also written books about you know slave drivers and whatsoever. If you are good at your job you will definitely get recognized. You can be a Team leader. We've got instances ... And even the women. Like if you think the NGOs line if you go to that. They train women for cottage industry. As in how to knit and all. Everything. Train them. Train them to speak English. It can be a very good cause. It can help so many women in India ... (27 December 2005)

Radhika's view of English in this comment is that it is a vocational skill. She supports English language education for the disadvantaged just as she does the work that NGOs do in training women for cottage industries. She sees the call center not as a 'slave driver', which she has read about in the newspapers, but as a provider of employment to the disadvantaged. Finally, she emphasizes the training that the national school system can provide, so as to link the school to this employment sector more closely.

Conclusions

This chapter has focused on the development of biliteracy in terms of how much is learned and what multilingual competencies are used for. It has shown that it is within the context of the New Work Order that English language literacy is situated in India. Thus the chapter has tried to make a connection between the domains of school and work. The word 'Sarvodaya', meaning welfare for all, is explained as one of the foundations of the chain of RSKV schools. Propagated by Mohandas Karamchand Gandhi, Sarvodaya refers to both the spiritual, intellectual and economic development of the individual in which access to dignified labor is integral. Schooling that is not vocationalized does not lead to Sarvodaya.

The reader is given an insight into a call center, which is an important workplace site in a globalizing India. I have also discussed the implications for identity inherent in the consumption of English. The idea of the agency of 'agents' in the call center and issues of linguistic racism have been discussed in detail. Literature that is critical of globalization processes shows individuals as agency-less; this is especially the way the developing world is portrayed in the literature. However Castells' (all three books) view, which is that in the new social order of globalization the individual still has agency which he/she exercises through renewed loyalty to language, religion and social groups, is borne out by my research. The agents in the XYZ call center are trying to break the cycle of social reproduction and English is a tool with which they are able to do so. They are able to tackle the 'tension between the Net and the Self' because of their syncretic identity and hybrid linguistic skills.

Chapter 7

Conclusions

'"India is the epicenter of the flat world" said Michael Cannon-Brookes, head of business development for China and India at IBM, referring to Thomas Friedman's book *The World is Flat*, which is about the leveling of barriers to global competition' (Bilefsky & Giridhadas, 2006). By the term 'flat world', Friedman's connotation is also that globalization creates more of a level playing field than that which exists currently in the world. As liberal academics have serious concerns about how egalitarian the processes of globalization actually are, this is indeed a controversial view. My book has offered an in-depth look at this epicenter in terms of bilingual education and the workplace. It has tried to showcase those in the urban disadvantaged community who are joining the globalizing workforce because of their new found access to the linguistic capital of English.

Friedman's book tells the good news about India – he shows an India where the IT sector is booming, new jobs are being created and numbers in the middle class are swelling. Though I think it is high time that this good news story reached international audiences, I cannot but be aware of haunting images from a developing country. 'Hundreds flee ethnic clashes in Assam: Hindi speakers leave in droves as the number of people killed by mobs and militants rises to 29'; the headline says it all (*The Straits Times*, 2003b). The article reports that clashes started when Assamese-speaking youth tried to prevent Hindi-speaking Bihari youth from taking recruitment tests for jobs at the state-run railways on 9 November 2003. This is the heart of darkness in India: ethnic and linguistic strife for access to employment by the disenfranchised millions. Yet, this heart of darkness is what the Western press, and in this case also the South East Asian press, has emphasized about India for decades. I have tried to tell a different story.

I do not believe that Indians who are learning English and working in call centers are slaves to the inexorable processes of globalization that they cannot control. On the contrary both Castells (1996/2000, 1997/2004, 1998/2000) and Amartya Sen emphasize the role of agency and voice as an integral part of this new social order. Castells shows how agency is manifested in the globalizing world through a rise in nationalist feeling, religious fundamentalism and loyalty to local communities and social groups. Amartya Sen's idea, stated very simply, for which he won the Nobel Prize in economics, is that democracy and freedom lead to economic development. Sen thinks that one of the reasons why India is able to be a major player in globalization is because it has a legacy of democratic freedoms. 'Freedoms are, thus, among the principal means as well as the primary ends of development' (Dreze & Sen, 2005: 4). In keeping with this spirit the urban disadvantaged in India have demanded access to the linguistic capital of English and are receiving it.

From a theoretical point of view this book has tried to give a different view of globalization: a view from a developing country that is benefiting from the processes of globalization. It has tried to persuade that literature critical of globalization, produced by mainly by historians and sociologists from developed countries, is not as nuanced as that produced by economists and anthropologists from India who might have a different story to tell. The book has also tried to substantiate some of these pro globalization claims through interviews with the management of a call center. In these interviews the management sees itself as an employment sector that is working in tandem with the government and the national school system. The management does not see itself as a sweatshop for the poor. No doubt the management can be faulted for these self-sustaining views, which support the proliferation of call centers. However the data in this book will help the reader see how difficult it is to take a stance if seen from the lens of the urban disadvantaged who need these jobs.

Theoretically the book has also tried to persuade that Mohandas Karamchand Gandhi was a social scientist with influential views on education that should not be swept under his spiritual aura. Gandhi should be considered as much a sociologist of education as Bourdieu and Bernstein who, like Gandhi, were concerned about the empowering aspect of education for the disadvantaged. In the context of this book Sarvodaya, meaning universal welfare, is access to the linguistic capital of English. India's economy began globalizing in 1991, which has created new sectors of employment, most of which require employees to know English. The urban disadvantaged are being prepared for these new sectors by the bilingual national education program in India. This book has presented an in-depth picture of a Hindi–English dual language program in a government school. In a country where unemployment is a social malaise it is not constructive to look at anti-globalization and anti-corporate propaganda produced from the liberal West. It is far more culturally contextualized to look at the opportunity and access to employment from Gandhi's viewpoint of 'Shram', which means dignified access to sustainable employment.

This book has emphasized the culture of pedagogy in India. Center-based language teaching methods like process writing, a student-centered classroom, extended oral response and other such pedagogies are out of place in the periphery classroom. In this enunciative space ancient pedagogies are still being used and the relationship between teacher and student does not allow a student-centered classroom. Also, though the purpose of English is integrative in center-based countries, it is instrumental in the developing world. However the problem is these culturally contextualized pedagogies are not able to provide communicative competence in English, which is the key demand of the globalizing workplace. The graduating students of the RSKV have to acquire this competence by paying high fees in the open linguistic market where English is extremely commodified.

As such there is urgent need for reform in changing interactional patterns in the classroom in alignment with teacher training. Yet, having established that prevailing pedagogies are culturally appropriate and show durability over the ages, there is the problem of how the strengths of such pedagogies can be retained while reforming them. The informal sector in India, which provides commodified English at high prices, does use pedagogies that inculcate communicative competence in English. Here the problem is that students are unable to sustain their new-found skills when the course is completed. The challenge for ELT in India is to integrate these pedagogies in the national school system so that the 12 years of English-medium instruction is adequate for many employment sectors in the workplace. This reform agenda will greatly benefit the disadvantaged who do not have the resources to buy English language skills outside the school system.

Despite these contradictions, the thrust of this book has been to show the empowering nature of bottom-up changes in English language policy within the Three Language Formula. The 6 extra years of ELT are highly valued by the students and their parents. These extra years do create the opportunity for teachers to change their pedagogic practice in the higher classes, like letting go of the scaffolding of the translation method and reserving it only for the primary classes. The story of empowerment has been linked to Gandhi's idea of a vocationalized school system and how the workplace is dealing with graduates of such a system.

Though this book is a study of bilingual education in India, the enunciative and physical spaces in this country of 1 billion are too vast for the

RSKV to be representative. For instance, rural India, where 75% of Indians live, is not even mentioned in this book. Here the system of education is totally different with multi-age, multi-grade classes, often held outdoors in the fields, conducted by secondary school students who have just graduated. Similarly the private school system, which is fee paying, is not the focus of this study. Also, the focus in this book is on how Hindi speakers learn English, which does not include speakers of non-Hindi languages. These omissions are entirely due to my limited background and that I do not have the expertise to deal with all these issues. Thus the reader is encouraged to take this as a limited narrative of bilingual education in urban North India amongst the disadvantaged.

Appendix 1: Non-scheduled Languages

Languages Not Specified in the V111TH Schedule

Language	*Number of persons speaking*
1. Adi	158,409
2. Anal	12,156
3. Angami	97,631
4. Ao	172,449
5. Arabic/Arbi	21,975
6. Bhili/Bhilodi	5,572,308
7. Bhotia	55,483
8. Bhumij	45,302
9. Bhihnupuriya	59,233
10. Bodo/boro	1,221,881
11. Chakesang	30,985
12. Chakru/Chokri	48,207
13. Chang	32,478
14. Coorgi/Kodagu	97,011
15. Deori	17,901
16. Dimasa	88,543
17. Dogri	89,681
18. English	178,598
19. Gadaba	28,158
20. Gangte	13,695
21. Garo	675,642

22. Gondi	2,124,852
23. Halabi	534,313
24. Halam	29,322
25. Hmar	65,204
26. Ho	949,216
27. Jatapu	25,730
28. Juang	16,858
29. Kabui	68,925
30. Karbi/Mikir	366,229
31. Khandeshi	973,709
32. Kharia	225,556
33. Khasi	912,283
34. Khezha	13,004
35. Khiemnungan	23,544
36. Khond/Khondh	220,783
37. Kinnauri	61,794
38. Kisan	162,088
39. Koch	26,179
40. Koda/Kara	28,200
41. Kolami	98,281
42. Kom	13,548
43. Konda	17,864
44. Konyak	137,722
45. Korku	466,073
46. Korwa	27,485
47. Koya	270,994
48. Kui	641,662
49. Kuki	58,263
50. Kurukh/Oraon	1,426,618

51. Lahauli	22,027
52. Lahnda	27,386
53. Lakher	22,947
54. Lalung	33,746
55. Lepcha	39,342
56. Liangmei	27,478
57. Limbu	28,174
58. Lotha	85,802
59. Lushai/Mizo	538,842
60. Malto	108,148
61. Mao	77,810
62. Maram	10,144
63. Maring	15,268
64. Miri/Mishing	390,583
65. Mishmi	29,000
66. Mogh	28,135
67. Monpa	43,226
68. Munda	413,894
69. Mundari	861,378
70. Nicobarese	26,261
71. Nissi/Dafla	173,791
72. Nocte	30,441
73. Paite	49,237
74. Parji	44,001
75. Pawi	15,346
76. Phom	65,350
77. Pochury	11,231
78. Rabha	139,365
79. Rengma	37,521

80. Sangtam	47,461
81. Santali	5,216,325
82. Savara	273,168
83. Sema	166,157
84. Sherpa	16,105
85. Tangkhul	101,841
86. Tangsa	28,121
87. Thado	107,992
88. Tibetan	69,416
89. Tripuri	694,940
90. Tulu	1,552,259
91. Vaiphei	26,185
92. Wancho	39,600
93. Yimchungre	47,227
94. Zeliang	35,097
95. Zemi	22,634
96. Zou	15,966

(From Bose, 1998, p. 152)

Appendix 2: 15-day Training Schedule for a Call Center

Unit	Topic	Duration
Day 1 Unit 1	Introduction to training • Ice breaker • Expectations • Ground Rules • Objectives of Foundations of Voice Training (FVT) training	1 Hr
Unit 2	Hear me speak • Trainees to speak on creative topics given by the trainer • Trainer to identify areas of improvement and provide feedback	4 Hrs
Unit 3	Introduction to the Accent • What is Neutralization of Accent • Why is it important • Role of Accent in BPO • Overview of different regional accents	2 Hrs
Day 2 Unit 1	Rate of Speech • Mouthing and Whispering • Recording the words per minute on a daily basis • Breathing and Jaw exercises • Mirror face Game	2 Hrs
Unit 2	Introduction to Vowel sounds • Jaw movement exercises • Audio Tapes to introduce the trainees to British Speech. • Introducing primary Vowel sounds using the audio tapes to trainees	5 Hrs

Unit	Topic	Duration
	• Activities to practise vowel sounds laying stress on the differences from Native Indian languages • Reading Practice using Vowel sounds	
Day 3 Unit 1	Consonants • Introduce the sounds from the phonemic chart • Comparison of the Indian and neutral sounds • Consonant drills • Tongue twisters • Audio Tapes to introduce the trainees to British Speech focusing on consonant sounds • Practise reading contemporary poetry using the sounds they have learnt.	5 Hrs
Unit 2	Rate of speech • How it affects our communication ability? • Free speech exercises	2 Hrs
Day 4	Syllable Stress & Rhythm • Syllable stress & its importance: Rules & Practice exercises • Word Stress & it's importance : Rules & Practice exercises • Rhythm & Intonation • Tongue Twisters : Practise sounds learnt& jaw movement exercises • Difference in pronunciations of some common words used in the UK & USA • Contractions & reductions • Listen & learn: Practise activities to facilitate application of things learnt during the day. This is clubbed with listening to audio tapes to reinforce information learnt	7 Hrs

Unit	Topic	Duration
Day 5	Accents across the UK • Differing sounds & pronunciation • Introduction to colloquial / Idioms & commonly used phrases in Different parts of the UK • British Slang • British American word contrasts • Recap & Test	7 Hrs
Day 6	Listen & learn • Play video & audio versions of Regional Accents • Test comprehension • Discuss response styles in terms of voice & words used • Reading passages of client related information • Reading with appropriate stress, intonation , pace & correct pronunciations • Comprehension & Extempore speaking on client centred & industry related topics. • Trainees to make verbal presentations on client related topics given to them. & record their voices to note improvement. • Indianisms and Basic Grammatical errors based on class needs.	7 Hrs
Day 7	Customer Service & Effective Communication • Theoretical discussion with presentations pertaining to : • The service concept • Importance of customer orientation in the BPO industry • Overview of Vital Customer service skills • Empathy: concept & activities to practise • Questioning skills: concept & activities to practise	7 Hrs

Unit	Topic	Duration
	• Acknowledgement & Word Choice: concept & activities to practise • Building rapport: concept & activities to practise • Listening skills: concept & activities to practise • Call Control	
Day 8	Customer Service in action • Recap of skills acquired • Customer service voice skit to be presented by trainees to display customer centricity through good & bad examples of daily life • Service NO: concept & activities • Attitude : Concept & Activities • Ownership, Reassurance & Responsibility: concept & activities • Telephone handling skills	7 Hrs
Day 9	• Revision of sounds , colloquial idioms & commonly mispronounced process related words • Pronunciation of county names & common British first & Family names • Behavioural style at the workplace & acceptable Etiquette • Watch a British movie: practise sounds; test for listening & comprehension & gauge cultural nuances.	7 Hr
Day 10	Speech & Vocabulary Enhancement • Reading Practise from eminent British authors: Passages & scripts throwing light upon the culture& enabling development of trainee vocabulary. • Vocabulary building using process related words & customer service. Trainer to give trainees scenarios which they need to enact in pairs.& use their creative thinking ability. • Revision of sounds , colloquial idioms & commonly mispronounced process related words	7 Hrs

Unit	Topic	Duration
Day 11	Mock calls • Trainees to combine their voice skills with customer service & practise various scenarios related to their process. They are given feedback on tackling different situations given to them in by different mock customers to prepare them for various situations.	7 Hrs
Day 12	Mock calls • Trainees to combine their voice skills with customer service & practise various scenarios related to their process. They are given feedback on tackling different situations given to them in by different mock customers to prepare them for various situations.	7 Hrs
Day 13	Mock calls • Trainees to combine their voice skills with customer service & practise various scenarios related to their process. They are given feedback on tackling different situations given to them in by different mock customers to prepare them for various situations.	7 Hrs
Day 14	Mock calls • Trainees to combine their voice skills with customer service & practise various scenarios related to their process. They are given feedback on tackling different situations given to them in by different mock customers to prepare them for various situations.	7 Hrs
Day 15	• Relaxation exercises • Final assessment & Feedback	7 Hr

Appendix 3: Photos

Class 12, English period

Primary Wing of the RSKV on a Saturday morning

Entrance to the school: a biliterate text

Saying by Mohandas Karamchand Gandhi on classroom door: "Work is worship, duty is prayer"

Bibliography

Aggarwal, J.C. (2000) *Educational Reforms in India for the 21st Century*. New Delhi: Shipra Publications.

Alexander, R. (2000) *Culture and Pedagogy: International Comparisons in Primary Education*. Massachusetts: Blackwell.

Annamalai, E. (2001) *Managing Multilingualism in India: Political and Linguistic Manifestations*. Vol. 8 in R. Singh and P. Dasgupta (eds) Language and Development series. New Delhi: Sage.

Appadurai, A. (1996) *Modernity at Large: Cultural Dimensions of Globalization*. Vol. 1 of Public Worlds. Minneapolis: University of Minnesota Press.

Appadurai, A. (2000) Grassroots globalization and the research imagination. *Public Culture* 12 (1), 1–19.

Baker, C. (2006) *Foundations of Bilingual Education and Bilingualism*. Clevedon: Multilingual Matters.

Barber, B.R. (1996) *Jihad vs McWorld: How Globalism and Tribalism are Reshaping the World*. New York: Random House.

Bhagwati, J. (2004) *In Defense of Globalization*. Oxford: Oxford University Press.

Bhatia, T.K. and Ritchie, W.C. (2004) Bilingualism in the global media and advertising. In T.K. Bhatia and W.C. Ritchie (eds) *The Handbook of Bilingualism* (pp. 513–545). Oxford: Blackwell Publishing.

Bhattacharya, S., Bara, J. and Yagati, C.R. (eds) (2003) *Educating the Nation: Documents on the Discourse of National Education in India 1880–1920*. New Delhi: Kanishka and Jawaharlal Nehru University.

Bilefsky, D. and Giridhadas, A. (2006) China and India take rival paths. *International Herald Tribune* 25 January, 1.

Block, D. and Cameron, D. (ed.) (2002) *Globalization and Language Teaching*. London: Routledge.

Bloom, A. (1987) *The Closing of the American Mind: How Higher Education Has Failed Democracy and Impoverished the Souls of Today's Students*. New York: Simon and Schuster.

Bose, A. (1998) *Demographic Diversity of India: 1991 Census, State and District Level Data*. New Delhi: B.R. Publishing Corporation.

Bourdieu, P. and Passeron, J.C. (1977) *Reproduction in Education, Society and Culture*. London: Sage.

Brass, P.R. (1990) Language problems. In P.R. Brass (ed.) *The Politics of India Since Independence* (pp. 135–168). Cambridge: Cambridge University Press.

Brutt-Griffler, J. (2002) *World English: A Study of its Development*. Clevedon: Multilingual Matters.

Business Week/Asian Edition (2003) The rise of India: And what it means for the global economy. 8 December.

Cameron, D. (2000) Styling the worker: Gender and the commodification of language in the globalized service economy. *Journal of Sociolinguistics* 4 (3): 323–347.

Canagarajah, S.A. (1995) The political economy of code choice in a 'revolutionary society': Tamil–English bilingualism in Jaffna, Sri Lanka. *Language in Society* 24 (2), 187–212.

Canagarajah, S.A. (1996) Functions of code-switching in ESL classrooms: Socialising bilingualism in Jaffna. *Journal of Multilingual and Multicultural Development* 13 (1–2), 173–195.

Canagarajah, S.A. (1999) *Resisting Linguistic Imperialism in English Teaching*. Oxford: Oxford University Press.

Canagarajah, S.A. (2001) Constructing hybrid postcolonial subjects: Codeswitching in Jaffna classrooms. In M. Heller and M. Martin-Jones (eds) *Contemporary Studies in Linguistics and Education* (pp. 193–212). Westport: Ablex Publishing.

Canagarajah, S.A. (2002) Globalization, methods, and practice in periphery classrooms. In D. Block and D. Cameron (eds) *Globalization and Language Teaching* (pp. 134–151). London: Routledge.

Carspecken, P.F. (1996) *Critical Ethnography in Educational Research: A Theoretical and Practical Guide*. New York and London: Routledge.

Castells, M. (1996/2000) *The Rise of the Network Society, The Information Age: Economy, Society and Culture* (Vol. I, 2nd edn). Oxford: Blackwell Publishers.

Castells, M. (1997/2004) *The Power of Identity, The Information Age: Economy, Society and Culture* (Vol. II, 2nd edn). Oxford: Blackwell Publishers.

Castells, M. (1998/2000) *The End of the Millennium, The Information Age: Economy, Society and Culture* (Vol. III, 2nd edn). Oxford: Blackwell Publishers.

CBSE (nd) *Interact in English: Literature Reader for English Course (Communicative)*. New Delhi: CBSE.

Cenoz, J. and Gorter, D. (2006) Linguistic landscape and minority languages. *International Journal of Multilingualism* 3, 67–80.

Chatterjee, S. and Somayaji, C. (2005) Business Asia. 'Outsourcing boom swells profit at Wipro.' *International Herald Tribune* 20 October, B1.

Clark, P. (2003) Culture and classroom reform: The case of the District Primary Education Project, India. *Comparative Education* 39 (1), 27–44.

Conrad, A.W. (1996) The international role of English: The state of the discussion. In J. Fishman, A.W. Conrad and A. Rubal-Lopez (eds) *Post-Imperial English: Status Change in Former British and American Colonies, 1940–1990* (pp. 13–36). Berlin: Mouton de Gruyter.

Cope, B. and Kalantzis, M. (2000) (eds) *Multiliteracies: Literacy Learning and the Design of Social Futures*. London: Routledge.

Cummins, J. (2000) *Language, Power and Pedagogy: Bilingual Children in the Crossfire*. Clevedon: Multilingual Matters.

DasGupta, J. (1970) *Language Conflict and National Development: Group Politics and National Language Policy in India*. Bombay: Oxford University Press.

DasGupta, J. (1977) Language associations in India. In B. Jernudd, J. DasGupta, J. Fishman and C.A. Ferguson (eds) *Language Planning Processes* (pp. 181–195). The Hague: Mouton.

Delhi: Human Development Report (2006) *Partnerships for Progress*. New Delhi: Oxford University Press.

Delpit, L.D. (2001) The silenced dialogue: Power and pedagogy in educating other people's children. In K. Halasek and N.P. Highberg (eds) *Landmark Essays on Basic Writing* (pp. 83–101). New Jersey: Lawrence Erlbaum Associates.

Dor, D. (2004) From Englishization to imposed multilingualism: Globalization, the internet, and the political economy of the linguistic code. *Public Culture* 16 (1), 97–118.

Dreze, J. and Sen, A. (2005) *India: Development and Participation*. New Delhi: Oxford University Press.

Drucker, P.F. (1993) *Post Capitalist Society*. Oxford: Butterworth–Heinemann.

Dua, H.R. (1996) The spread of English in India: Politics of language conflict and language power. In J. Fishman, A.W. Conrad and A. Rubal-Lopez (eds) *Post-Imperial English: Status Change in Former British and American Colonies, 1940–1990* (pp. 557–589). Berlin: Mouton de Gruyter.

Freire, P. (1971) *Pedagogy of the Oppressed* (M. Bergman, trans.) New York: Herder and Herder.

Friedman, T. (2005) *The World is Flat: A Brief History of the Globalized World in the 21st Century*. London: Allen Lane.

Gal, S. (1993) Diversity and contestation in linguistic ideologies: German speakers in Hungary. *Language in Society* 22, 337–359.

Gandhi, M.K. (1953) *Towards New Education*. Ahmedabad: Navajivan Publishing House.

Gandhiji (1955) *Sarvodaya*. Ahmedabad: Navjeevan Publication Temple.

Gandhiji (1957) *My Experiments with Truth or Autobiography*. Ahmedabad: Navjeevan Publication Temple.

Gandhiji (1967) *The History of Resistance in South Africa*. Ahmedabad: Navjeevan Publication Temple.

Gee, J., Hull, G. and Lankshear, C. (1996) *The New Work Order: Behind the Language of the New Capitalism*. Sydney: Allen and Unwin.

Giddens, A. (1990) *The Consequences of Modernity*. Stanford: Stanford University Press.

Giddens, A. (2001) Dimensions of globalization. In S. Seidman and J.C. Alexander (eds) *The New Social Theory Reader* (pp. 244–252). London: Routledge.

Goh, Y.S. (2000) The rise of global Mandarin: Opportunities and challenges. In W.K. Ho and C. Ward (eds) *Language in the Global Context: Implications for the Language Classroom*. Singapore: RELC.

Government of India (1993) Learning without burden: Report of the National Advisory committee Appointed by the Ministry of Human Resource Development. New Delhi: Department of Education.

Govinda, R. (ed.) (2002) *India Education Report: A Profile of Basic Education*. New Delhi: Oxford University Press, NIEPA and UNESCO.

Hannum, E. and Fuller, B. (eds) (2006) *Children's Lives and Schooling Across Societies*. Vol. 15 in Research in Sociology of Education. Amsterdam: Elsevier.

Hornberger, N.H. (1990a) Teacher Quechua use in bilingual and non-bilingual classrooms of Puno, Peru. In R. Jacobson and C. Faltis (eds) *Language Distribution Issues in Bilingual Schooling* (pp. 163–174). Clevedon: Multilingual Matters.

Hornberger, N.H. (1990b) Creating successful learning contexts for bilingual literacy. *Teachers College Record* 92 (2), 212–229.

Hornberger, N.H. (2000) Multilingual literacies, literacy practices, and the continua of biliteracy. In M. Martin-Jones and K. Jones (eds) *Multilingual Literacies: Reading and Writing Different Worlds* (pp. 353–369). Philadelphia: John Benjamins.

Hornberger, N.H. (ed.) (2003) *Continua of Biliteracy: An Ecological Framework for Educational Policy, Research, and Practice in Multilingual Settings*. Clevedon: Multilingual Matters.

Hornberger, N.H. (2007) In A. Creese, P.W. Martin and N.H. Hornberger (eds) *Encyclopedia of Language and Education. Volume 9: Ecology of Language.* Berlin: Springer (forthcoming).

Hornberger, N.H. and Vaish, V. (2006) Multilingual language policy and school linguistic practice: Globalization and educational equity in South Africa, India and Singapore. Paper presented at *Sociolinguistics Symposium 16*, 5–8 July 2006. Limerick, Ireland.

International Herald Tribune (2003) Indians pin hopes on private schools and English. By A. Waldman. 18 November, 3.

International Herald Tribune (2004) Business Asia. 'A US front office for India's outsourcers'. By A. Mukerjee. 26 October, B2.

Jacobson, R. (1990) Allocating two languages as a key feature of a bilingual methodology. In R. Jacobson and C. Faltis (eds) *Language Distribution Issues in Bilingual Schooling* (pp. 3–18). Clevedon: Multilingual Matters.

Kachru, Y. (2006) Mixers lyricing in Hinglish: Blending and fusion in Indian pop culture. *World Englishes* 25 (22), 223–233.

Kamwangamalu, N.M. (1992) 'Mixers' and 'mixing': English across cultures. *World Englishes* 11 (2/3), 173–181.

Kenner, C. (2004) *Becoming Biliterate: Young Children Learning Different Writing Systems.* Stoke-on-Trent: Trentham Books.

Kenner, C. and Kress, G. (2003) The multisemiotic resources of biliterate children. *Journal of Early Childhood Literacy* 3 (2), 179–202.

Kenner, C., Kress, G., Al-Khatib, H., Kam, R. and Tsai, K.-C. (2004) Finding the keys to biliteracy: How young children interpret different writing systems. *Language and Education* 18 (2), 124–144.

Khubchandani, L. (2003) Defining mother tongue education in plurilingual contexts. *Language Policy* 2, 239–254.

Kress, G. (2003) *Literacy in the New Media Age.* London: Routledge.

Krishnaswamy, N. and Burde, A. (1998) *The Politics of Indians' English: Linguistic Colonialism and the Expanding Empire.* New Delhi: Oxford University Press.

Kumar, K. (2005) *Political Agenda of Education: A Study of Colonialist and Nationalist Ideas* (2nd edn). New Delhi: Sage.

Kumaravadivelu, B. (1994) The Postmethod Condition: (E)merging strategies for second/foreign language teaching. *TESOL Quarterly* 28 (1), 27–48.

Kumaravadivelu, B. (2002) From coloniality to globality: (Re)visioning English language education in India. *Indian Journal of Applied Linguistics* 28 (2), 45–61.

Ladousa, C. (2002) Advertising in the periphery: Languages and schools in a North Indian City. *Language in Society* 31, 213–242.

Lankshear, C. (1997) *Changing Literacies.* Philadelphia: Open University Press.

Lankshear, C. and Knobel, M. (2003) *New Literacies: Changing Knowledge and Classroom Learning.* Philadelphia: Open University Press.

Lin, A.Y. (2001) Symbolic domination and bilingual classroom practices in Hong Kong. In M. Heller and M. Martin-Jones (eds) *Voices of Authority: Education and Linguistic Difference* (pp. 139–169). London: Ablex.

Mahapatra, B.P. (1990) A demographic appraisal of multilingualism in India. In D.P. Pattanayak (ed.) *Multilingualism in India* (pp. 1–15). Clevedon: Multilingual Matters.

Martin-Jones, M. and Jones, K. (eds) (2000) *Multilingual Literacies: Reading and Writing in Different Worlds.* Philadelphia: John Benjamins.

McCall, C. (2003) Language dynamics in the bi- and multilingual workplace. In R. Bayle and S.R. Schecter (eds) *Language Socialization in Bilingual and Multilingual Societies* (pp. 235–251). Clevedon: Multilingual Matters.

Mehrotra, R.R. (1993) The First Congress of Hindi. In J.A. Fishman (ed.) *The Earliest Stage of Language Planning: The 'First Congress' Phenomenon* (pp. 117–129). Berlin: Mouton de Gruyter.

Ministry of Information and Broadcasting (2000) *India 2000: A Reference Annual.* Ministry of Information and Broadcasting, Government of India.

Mohanan, T. (1994) *Argument Structure in Hindi.* Stanford: Center for the Study of Language and Information Publications.

Mohanty, A.K. (2006) Multilingualism of the unequals and predicaments of education in India: Mother tongue or other tongue? In O. Garcia, T. Skutnabb-Kangas and M.E. Torres-Guzman (eds) *Imagining Multilingual Schools: Languages in Education and Glocalization* (pp. 262–283). Clevedon: Multilingual Matters

Nandy, A. (1983) *The Intimate Enemy: Loss and Recovery of Self under Colonialism.* New Delhi: Oxford University Press.

Nandy, A. (1995) *The Savage Freud and Other Essays on Possible and Retrievable Selves.* New Delhi: Oxford University Press.

NCERT (1989) *Exploring Environment: A Textbook for Class V.* By S. Bhattacharya and H.L. Sharma. New Delhi: NCERT.

NCERT (2002) *English With A Purpose: Textbook for Class XI.* S. Sahoo and V.K. Bajpai (eds). New Delhi: NCERT.

NCERT (2003a) *Impressions: Supplementary Reader for Class XII. Core English.* K. Kapur and R. Dixit (eds). New Delhi: NCERT.

NCERT (2003b) *Working with English: Workbook for Class XII.* By J.P. Kaushal. New Delhi: NCERT.

NCERT (2003c) *Steps to English: Textbook for Class X.* S. Sahoo (ed.). New Delhi: NCERT.

NCERT (2003d) *English with a Purpose: Textbook for Class XII. (Core Course).* R. Dave (ed.). New Delhi: NCERT.

Pahl, K. (ed.) (2006) *Travel Notes from the New Literacy Studies: Instances of Practice.* Clevedon, Multilingual Matters.

Pattanayak, D.P. (1986) Language, politics, region formation, and regional planning. In E. Annamalai, B. Jernudd and J. Rubin (eds) *Language Planning: Proceedings of an Institute* (pp. 18–43). CIIL: Mysore.

Pennycook, A. (1998) *English and the Discourses of Colonialism.* London: Routledge.

Pennycook, A. (2000) Language, ideology and hindsight: Lessons from colonial language policies. In T. Ricento (ed.) *Ideology, Politics and Language Policies: Focus on English* (pp. 107–119). Philadelphia: John Benjamins.

Phillipson, R. (1992) *Linguistic Imperialism.* Oxford: Oxford University Press.

Phillipson, R. (2006) Language policy and linguistic imperialism. In T. Ricento (ed.) *An Introduction to Language Policy: Theory and Method.* London: Blackwell Publishing.

Phillipson, R. and Skutnabb-Kangas, T. (1997) Linguistic human rights and English in Europe. *World Englishes* 16, 27–43.

Phillipson, R. and Skutnabb-Kangas, R. (1999) Englishisation: One dimension of globalization. *AILA Review* 13, 19–36.

Pieterse, J.N. (2004) *Globalization & Culture: Global Melange.* New York, Rowman & Littlefield Publishers Inc.

Pollack, A. (2005) Biotech shifts jobs offshore: Life Science research is outsourced to Asia. *International Herald Tribune* 25 February, 15.

Prabhu, R.K. and Rao, U.R. (2003) *Mahatma Gandhi ke Vichaar*. Ahmedabad: Navjeevan Book Trust.

PROBE (1999) *Public Report on Basic Education in India*. New Delhi: Oxford University Press.

Putnam, R.D. (1995) Bowling alone: America's declining social capital. *Journal of Democracy* 6, 65–78.

Ramanathan, V. (2005) *The English–Vernacular Divide: Postcolonial Language Politics and Practice*. Clevedon: Multilingual Matters.

Ramanathan, V. (2006a) The vernacularization of English: Crossing global currents to re-dress West-based TESOL. *Critical Inquiry in Language Studies* 3 (2&3), 131–146.

Ramanathan, V. (2006b) Gandhi, non-cooperation, and socio-civic education in Gujarat, India: Harnessing the vernaculars. *Journal of Language Identity and Education* 5 (3), 229–250.

Rampal, A. (2007) *Bridging the Orality-Literacy Gap: Education For and By All. Redesigning Pedagogy: Culture, Knowledge & Understanding*. 28–30 May 2007, Singapore.

Rampton, B. (1995) *Crossings: Language and Ethnicity Among Adolescents*. Longman: London and New York.

Reich, R.B. (1991) *The Work of Nations: Preparing Ourselves for 21st Century Capitalism*. New York: Knopf.

Ritchie, W.C. and Bhatia, T.K. (2004) Social and psychological factors in language mixing. In T.K. Bhatia and W.C. Ritchie (eds) *The Handbook of Bilingualism* (pp. 336–352). Oxford: Blackwell Publishing.

Roy, S. (2003) Bilingualism and standardization in a Canadian call centre: Challenges for a linguistic minority community. In R. Bayley and S.R. Schecter (eds) *Language Socialization in Bilingual and Multilingual Societies* (pp. 269–286). Clevedon: Multilingual Matters.

Ruskin, J. (1985) *Unto This Last and Other Writings*. C. Wilmer (ed.). London: Penguin.

Said, E.W. (1978). *Orientalism*. New York: Vintage Books.

Schiffman, H. (1996) Indian linguistic culture and the genesis of language policy in the subcontinent. In H. Schiffman, *Linguistic Culture and Language Policy: The Politics of Language* (pp. 148–173). London: Routledge.

Sen, A. (2004) How to judge globalism. In F.J. Lechner and J. Boli (eds) *The Globalization Reader* (pp. 16–22). Oxford: Blackwell Publishing.

Shiva, V. (2000/2004). Ecological balance in an era of globalization. In F.J. Lechner and J. Boli (eds) *The Globalization Reader* (2nd edn). Oxford: Blackwell Publishing.

Shome, R. (2006) Thinking through the diaspora: Call centres, India and the new politics of hybridity. *International Journal of Cultural Studies* 9 (1), 105–124.

Sinha, S.K. (2003) Career brakes: Call centers. *Outlook: The Weekly Newsmagazine* XLIII (40), 56–58.

Skutnabb-Kangas, T. (2000) *Linguistic Genocide in Education, or World Wide Diversity and Human Rights?* Mahwah, NJ: Lawrence Erlbaum Associates.

Skutnabb-Kangas, T. (2003) Linguistic diversity and biodiversity: The threat from killer languages. In C. Mair (ed.) *The Politics of English as a World Language: New Horizons in Postcolonial Cultural Studies*. Amsterdam: Rodopi.

Soh, F. (2005) Why Asia's local-language media will grow and grow: Globalization of the local. *The Straits Times* 11 September, 29.

Spring, J. (2001) India: Education, human rights, and the global flow. In J. Spring (ed.) *Globalization and Educational Rights: An Intercivilizational Analysis* (pp. 115–152). Mahwah: Lawrence Erlbaum Associates.

Srivastava, R.N. (1979) Language movements against Hindi as an official language. In E. Annamalai (ed.) *Language Movements in India* (pp. 80–90). Mysore: CIIL.

Street, B. (1995) *Social Literacies: Critical Approaches to Literacy in Development, Ethnography and Education*. London: Longman.

Street, B. (2001) *Literacy and Development: Ethnographic Perspectives*. London: Routledge.

Straits Times, The (2003a) Big job exodus: 4000 British posts will be moved to Asia. Saturday, 18 October, 7.

Straits Times, The (2003b) Hundreds flee ethnic clashes in Assam: Hindi speakers leave in droves as the number of people killed by mobs and militants rises to 29. Friday, 21 November, A13.

Stromquist, N.P. (2002) *Education in a Globalized World: The Connectivity of Economic Power, Technology, and Knowledge*. New York: Rowman & Littlefield Publishers.

Tamatea, L. (2006) Gandhian education in Bali: globalization and cultural diversity in a time of fundamentalisms. *Compare* 36 (2), 213–228.

Tickoo, M.L. (1996) English in Asian bilingual education: From hatred to harmony. *Journal of Multilingual and Multicultural Development* 17 (2–4), 225–240.

Vaish, V. (2004) Vidyashakti: Biliteracy and empowerment in India, the continua of biliteracy in action. Unpublished Ph.D. dissertation, University of Pennsylvania.

Vaish, V. (2005) A peripheral view of English as a language of decolonization in post-colonial India. *Language Policy* 4 (2), 187–206.

Varshney, H.K. (2002) Inter-state gender disparity in literacy rates – A look at census data (1991 & 2001). *Journal of Educational Planning and Administration* XVI (42001), 537–551.

Wallerstein, I. (1974) *The Modern World – System I: Capitalist Agriculture and the Origins of the European World-Economy in the Sixteenth Century. Studies in Social Discontinuity*. San Diego: Harcourt Brace Jovanovich, Publishers.

Wallerstein, I. (1980) *The Modern World – System II: Mercantilism and the Consolidation of the European World-Economy, 1600–1750. Studies in Social Discontinuity*. New York: Harcourt Brace Jovanovich, Publishers.

Wallerstein, I. (1989) *The Modern World – System III: The Second Era of Great Expansion of the Capitalist World-Economy, 1730–1840. Studies in Social Discontinuity*. San Diego: Harcourt Brace Jovanovich, Publishers.

Warschauer, M. (2002) Languages.com: The Internet and linguistic purism. In I. Snyder (ed.) *Silicon Literacies: Communication, Innovation and Education in the Electronic Age* (pp. 62–75). London: Routledge.

Warschauer, M., El Said, G.R. and Zohry, A. (2002) Language choice online: Globalization and identity in Egypt. *Journal of Computer Mediated Communication* 7 (4). Accessed 01.06.

Wright, M.W. (2001) More than just chanting: Multilingual literacies, ideology and teaching methodologies in rural Eritrea. In B. Street (ed.) *Literacy and Development: Ethnographic Perspectives* (pp. 61–78). London: Routledge.

Young, R. (2001) *Postcolonialism: An Historical Introduction*. Malden: Blackwell Publishers.

Webography

http://www.bbcHindi.com
http://www.ciil.org
http://www.CNNArabic.com
http://www.censusindia.net/results/provindia1.html
http://www.constitution.org/cons/india
www.censusindia.gov.in/Census_Data_2001/National_Summary/National_
Summary_DataPage.aspx
http://www.raga.com
http://www.zee-tv.com/Zee_Serial.aspx?zsid=56